UNCOVERED

WHY BECOMING LESS
BECAME EVERYTHING

Vance Johnson

with *New York Times* bestselling author Shirley Jump

PUBLISHING

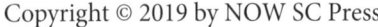

Copyright © 2019 by NOW SC Press

All rights reserved. No part of this publication may be reproduced, distributed, or transmitted in any form or by any means, including photocopying, recording, or other electronic or mechanical methods, without the prior written permission of the publisher, except in the case of brief quotations embodied in critical reviews and certain other noncommercial uses permitted by copyright law. For permission requests, write to the publisher, addressed "Attention: Permissions Coordinator," via the website below.

All Bible verses are from the New International Version, unless otherwise noted.

1.888.5069-NOW
PublishWithNOW.com
@nowscpress

Ordering Information:

Quantity sales. Special discounts are available on quantity purchases by corporations, associations, and others. For details, contact the publisher at the address above.

Orders by U.S. trade bookstores and wholesalers. Please contact: NOW SC Press: Tel: (888) 5069-NOW or visit PublishWithNOW.com.

Printed in the United States of America

First Printing, 2019

ISBN: 978-1-7326611-1-0

Cover photo by Rob Mason

A portion of the proceeds from this book goes to support Vance Inspires, a charity providing resources for those in recovery.

Dedication

To my father; I forgive you and I love you. The battle isn't with the person, it's the spiritual war going on that causes people to fight each other. Love covers a multitude of sins and frees us from wanting to self-medicate.

To my son, Vaughn. Forever and always, this is for you.

And most of all, to the Lord who saved me when I was lost.

To Oglethorpe, Inc., for supporting me and recovery efforts nationwide. May more people find hope and recovery.

Contents

Foreword

I've known brother Vance Johnson since 1984. During our college days, we were elected to participate in and be roommates in the East/West Shrine game. We were both seniors that year, and both invited to play in front of NFL scouts in California. We hit it off right away, and during the days we were staying there, we got to know each other. We talked about our childhoods and our dreams of becoming something great.

We vowed right then and there to be friends, to support each other in this game, and to stay friends after we were drafted. In the game, I passed the ball to him as often as I could, knowing the scouts were watching him. Coach Edwards from BYU called a sweep pass back to the quarterback, and Vance threw me a touchdown.

We both also participated at the NFL combine in Arizona. There, Vance was just as generous and eager to help out a friend. He wanted to see me succeed, too, and tried to give me opportunities to shine every time we were on the field. When the draft picks were announced, Vance was picked early on. He called me, and as we were talking on the phone, the Philadelphia Eagles drafted me. I think he was more excited than I was, because he was so grateful to see his friend succeed. Just as we had promised, we remained friends, up to and long after the draft.

We drifted apart for several years, as he went off to play with the Broncos, and I played for the Eagles. It wasn't until the last few years that we got in contact with each other again. The Vance I knew in those college days had been through an incredible journey, and we found that once again, we shared so much in common. My two-and-a-half-year-old son drowned, and Vance lost his son Vaughn, awful tragedies that meant the two of us understood each other's pain. We were both passionate about the Lord, and about helping other people.

What I see when I look at Vance Johnson is truth. He is who he says he is—a passionate, strong, courageous man of God, who owns his past and every mistake he made. He is genuine and real, and no longer hides behind the uniform and fame of the NFL.

I've been a pastor for 14 years, and now Vance is an evangelist, calling others to believe in Jesus. In college, I was the quarterback, and he was the wide receiver, carrying the ball down the field. It's amazing that we are both in ministry. Now it's all about the Word of God. Instead of football, it's now the message of God. As we did long ago, we have come together as friends, supporting each other and showing those around us the way out of darkness. I know the Lord is working in Vance, and I am so proud to call him a friend.

His book is one that will hopefully open your eyes to the complexities of addiction, and to the power of faith in recovery. Vance is true to his story, to his faith, and to his mission, and I know you will find hope and strength in his story.

In college, we played a game that lasted a few years. But now, as we each coach the lost through the Gospel, it's now about an everlasting life with the One who created us all.

Dr. Randall Cunningham
#12, Quarterback, Philadelphia Eagles, 1985-1995
Pastor, Remnant Ministries Church, Las Vegas

Vance Johnson is a true man of God and his story in his new book, *Uncovered*, should inspire whoever reads it. I have worked in the addiction and recovery world for many years and crossed paths with numerous celebrities who had recovered but were not willing to open up their lives to help battle this epidemic, but not Vance! Vance has not only shared every detail of his past life as an addict but has dedicated himself and his future to helping others suffering from this deadly brain disease This former NFL Superstar is now on the frontlines of the war on addiction, working tirelessly to help others in need across this entire nation. Oglethorpe Inc. is so proud to have the opportunity to partner with this true believer as we open The Vance Johnson Recovery Center in Las Vegas and implement his Christian Recovery Program throughout many of our other facilities.

John Picciano
CEO/ Managing Partner
Oglethorpe, Inc.

One

Admit

For I know that good itself does not dwell in me, that is, in my sinful nature. For I have the desire to do what is good, but I cannot carry it out. – Romans 7:18

Vance Johnson came home from playing in his first Super Bowl, sat in the dark of his bedroom closet, and tried to slit his wrists. He was twenty-three years old and, by all appearances, seemed to be on top of the world. No one knew he was a depressed, addicted, and desperate mess.

One of the "Three Amigos" recruited by Mike Shanahan for the Denver Broncos, the wide receiver had been drafted in the second round in the middle of his junior year of college. He was the thirty-first pick overall out of three hundred and sixty-eight players. He'd always been an incredible athlete, and even qualified as an alternate for the Olympics in the long jump. When he was a kid, he raced his cousins for a quarter a race and never, ever lost. He loved sports and had that rare natural ability coaches are always looking for. During his ten years with the Broncos, he went to the Super Bowl three times and set three franchise records for punt returns.

A few days earlier, he was standing on the sidelines at the Rose Bowl stadium in Pasadena, California, where the Broncos were playing the New York Giants in Super Bowl XXI. That moment was the pinnacle, the moment he had dreamed of all his life, the moment he thought would change everything. "I remember standing on the sidelines of the stadium, seeing the massive crowds, listening to the national anthem. All of a sudden, I was six years old, standing on the sidelines of an NFL game, dreaming of this moment. I started crying, right there at the Super Bowl, thinking, *I made it, oh my God, I made it.* That day, I played my heart out and gave it my all. But then I went home, and there was…nothing." Caught in a dark, bottomless pit of despair, he made the first of many attempts to end his life.

You hear that story and think *What? How could that be? He just played in the Super Bowl. How could anything be depressing after that?* To understand that moment in Vance's head, start by understanding how a troubled childhood impacts an adult, how addiction twists the words in the brain, and how depression can convince even the richest, most famous person (Anthony Bourdain, Robin Williams, and Kate Spade, to name just a few) that life isn't worth living.

"I had this voice in my head constantly saying *you should kill yourself,*" Vance said. That's all he could hear. All he could think, was that the world would be better off without him. His first marriage was falling apart, and he was already well on his way down a bumpy road of addiction to pills and alcohol. He'd struggled with self-esteem issues all his life and had always thought that once he reached the top of his game he would be okay. He wasn't. If anything, he was more depressed and more lost, which was what put him in that closet debating whether to keep living or take his own life. "That voice isn't the voice of God, it's the Devil telling you what to do. He disguises himself as your own voice, then takes those wounds that are deep inside you and uses them to convince you to make that first cut."

This wasn't the first time he contemplated suicide, nor would it be the last. "I thought of doing it often, for years. I always had many, many thoughts of dying by my own hands. But only three times or so did I actually physically harm myself with intent."

For years, Vance had numbed those thoughts and that voice inside his head with alcohol and prescription drugs, two things that seemed to come part and parcel with signing an NFL contract, along with entering into a world of parties, pain meds, and peer pressure. Growing up, Vance had never been a drinker. He'd seen how alcohol could turn his father into a raging bull and had spent more than one night with his mother searching local bars for his father—who was undoubtedly in the arms of another woman. His father had a hair trigger temper and regularly hit his wife for the slightest reason. When Vance was four, he and his sister were in the family car, heading to a family get together. His parents were arguing, and out of the blue his father hit his mother so hard blood spattered across the pale sedan's interior and speckled the windshield. Vance and his younger sister sat there frozen, traumatized and terrified.

This wasn't the first time he contemplated suicide, nor would it be the last.

Vance vowed, from a very early age, that he would never be that kind of man. Never hurt a woman. Never be an alcoholic. And for the duration of his childhood, high school, and college years, he kept that promise. He barely dated, for which the other kids call him gay because he had friendships with girls but not relationships. The other teenagers tried to get him to party, but he refused, becoming a loner who chose to spend his hours either in the gym or the art room.

All around him, he saw kids who had what he wanted—loving families, confidence in the classroom, girlfriends who adored them. Vance stuttered when he was young, so the thought of speaking aloud gave him panic attacks. He was the shy kid, standing apart against the wall and watching the world go by, dreaming of more. In his teens, he once left his own birthday party because he was too shy and too self-conscious to be the center of attention, even for one day.

In his senior year, Vance was at his school for a track meet when he saw a snippet of another person's life. There was a guy standing by the fence, watching the athletes on the track. A girl came up behind the young man. She wrapped her arms around his waist and, when he turned to smile at her, she whispered, "I love you." Vance watched them, envious and lost. He craved that kind of relationship, one with an unbreakable bond, a deep, abiding love that he could depend upon when the days got dark. But he had no frame of reference for how to build that connection, and deep down inside, he wondered if he was even worth that kind of love.

Even then, all the pieces of the jigsaw puzzle that led to his marital and addiction problems were falling into place: the multi-generational build-up created a damaged self-esteem, rootless existence, and an inability to maintain close relationships. Vance will tell you that his own choices put him where he is today but history also has an impact, something researchers are just now beginning to put together:

- In 2016, Michigan State University released a paper stating that a father's psychological state has a significant impact on his children.

- The Substance Abuse and Mental Health Services Administration (a division of the US Health and Human Services department) found that more than 12% of all children are living in a house where at least one parent has a substance abuse problem.

- The SAMHS 2017 report also stated that children who grow up with a parent who abuses drugs or alcohol have increased difficulty in academic, social, and relationship settings.

- In 2016, Harvard Medical School announced new findings linking parental/caregiver abuse of drugs or alcohol to a significantly higher risk of those same addictions in their children.

That means one in eight children are growing up with a parent who is an alcoholic or drug addict. Vance was one of that 12%, and it invaded every part of his childhood and adult life, as it had for his father before him.

Vance's father, the youngest of six children of a hard-working Christian woman, started running numbers for the gang leaders in Trenton, New Jersey almost as soon as he could walk. His own father (Vance's grandfather), a gambler and alcoholic, ended up dying on the railroad tracks. For minorities growing up in the forties and fifties, there were very, very few options for recovery groups or addiction support. Johnson's father found a quick path to making money and he took it. He spent his teenage years being chased by the cops and avoiding jail.

One in eight children are growing up with a parent who is an alcoholic or drug addict.

When he was twenty, the elder Johnson had lived out his nine lives with the Trenton police department. Arrested yet again, the judge gave him a choice: Go to jail or join the army. Vance's father chose the army. It was there, on leave, that he met Vance's mother, six years his junior, outside a James Brown concert. They talked for hours and he was smitten. That summer, she earned money picking cotton in the blazing Arizona heat for sixteen cents a day. When she returned to high school as a sophomore, her twenty-one-year old boyfriend walked across the gym floor and asked her to marry him. A year later, they moved back to Trenton and had their first child, a son.

Pretty quickly, Vance's father returned to the life he knew and the easy money he'd missed while on the U.S. Army's payroll. With gang life came alcohol and violence, both on the streets and at home. In an effort to get her husband away from that life, Vance's mother moved the family back to Arizona, but the cross-country relocation didn't change anything other than their address.

Vance's father had a temper that would explode without warning, leaving his petrified mother sobbing and cowering. In those days, there was no such thing as domestic violence shelters or hotlines. Vance's mother saw no way out of her situation and stayed, stuck financially and paralyzed emotionally. "My mom was always in the bedroom on her knees, crying and praying. She was the one going to church while my dad would go out to bars and come back with lipstick on his collar, smelling of perfume, looking like he was always having fun. I started to resent and hate my father, and most of all, hate my life. Then I got introduced to sports and that was where I found my escape. I knew the reality of what I lived and witnessed wasn't what I wanted, and I saw sports as a way to escape that."

Vance worked hard because he figured out early on that doing his best and pleasing his father eased the tension in the house. His father was his track and football coach for a few years, which made for a difficult dichotomy of burying the hatred Vance felt while respecting his father as a coach. "When I performed well on the field, life became less chaotic. I became the hero in the house," Vance explained. "Many kids in their adolescent years play a role. Some play the jokester, some play the hero, some kids just disappear and rebel. My role was to be the hero."

But in the off-season, the abuse started up again with a vengeance. Watching it was so traumatizing to Vance that he stayed away from girls, terrified to be in a relationship and discover he was like his father. Recent studies by the Grady Trauma Project, a research institute within Emory University in Atlanta, said that babies and young children exposed to domestic violence often end up developing PTSD that is as bad as what a soldier experiences after serving in combat. These children grow up watching the person who is supposed to love and protect the family hurt those very same people. The abuse creates chaos, uncertainty, and a war of love and hate inside the child.

As Vance grew taller, stronger, and more confident, he began to meet other role models, like his high school football coach, who showed him not all men hit women, and that responsible men showed up and did their job. When Vance's girlfriend broke up with him, he bailed on his track meet and hung out in the park, smoking weed with some other kids. Coach Brown kicked him off the team and told Vance the only way he could get back on was by apologizing to all of them for letting them down. "It was really hard to do, but I did it. Then Coach Brown said, 'Now that you've done that, apologize to the entire student assembly.' So I stood up in front of twenty-five hundred kids and apologized for my behavior. Coach Brown gave me tough constructive criticism but he also loved me like I was his own kid. He took me under his wing and was a great influence."

Coach Brown sat with him and talked to him about everything except for what Vance was going through at home. They talked about sports, college, and the coach's previous military life. Whenever Vance needed someone, Coach Brown was there. "I struggled with depression as a teenager, too, and people like Coach Brown are the only reason I didn't commit suicide."

As soon as Vance walked through the door at home, he stepped straight into hell. "I'd be in my bedroom when my dad came home. He'd be mad that I'd spent my time drawing, so he'd rip the pictures off the wall and throw them away. Or he'd be pissed off that I was in my bed when I had a track meet coming up, so he'd tell me to go run. Didn't matter what time it was—if he told me to go run, I did. I'd disappear into my head and run for a half an hour in the middle of the night just so I didn't have to be around the chaos at home."

> *The road to addiction is rarely an express lane.*

When he was sixteen, Vance walked in on his intoxicated father once again beating his mother. Vance had reached his breaking point. Vance ordered his father outside. He picked up a huge rock and held it over his father's head, threatening to kill him. His father dropped to his knees and begged his son to spare him. "I won't kill you," Vance replied, "but don't you *ever* touch her again."

The damage, however, was already done to young Vance's psyche, and the wounds that fed his doubts and despair were already beginning to open. The road to addiction is rarely an express lane. Many addicts choose a drug—alcohol, heroin, food, sex, codependency—to quiet the voices in their head that say they aren't good enough, they can't handle it, they deserve the punishment they've received, and most of all, that any other kind of existence is impossible. Like hundreds of others who have made the difficult journey crawling out of that pit of despair, Vance Johnson had a history that pushed him down when he should have been able to look up.

He had his first drink the day before the Broncos made their final cuts. He'd been playing in a game against the 49ers and bobbled a punt, sending the ball into the end zone and allowing them to score a touchdown. He was convinced his NFL career was over before it really got started, and when a friend on the team suggested they do some tequila shots, Vance decided to join them.

"As soon as I did the shot, I was like *whoa, what is this?* And that was it. I started drinking and never stopped." In fact, the prescription drug abuse and alcohol use would get so bad, Vance ended up in jail for vehicular assault, lost every dime he made in the NFL, blew through eight marriages, and ended up selling his Super Bowl rings at a pawn shop to pay his bills and support his habit.

Even as he walked away from his Broncos contract, sank into debt, ruined friendships and relationships, he kept telling himself he was fine, just fine; he had it all under control. Vance survived things that should have killed him, events recounted in this book, events that are almost unbelievable. "I was constantly searching for joy and fulfillment—in women, alcohol, and football. But the more I searched, the bigger that hole inside me got, because I couldn't fill it no matter what I did."

Then in 2007, his son Vaughn was killed in a motorcycle crash. A drunk driver ran a stop sign and plowed her SUV straight into Johnson's youngest son. Vaughn, a college student and aspiring football player like his father, died at the hospital. In a horrible ironic twist, the powerful demon of addiction that Johnson had been carrying around for decades took away one of the most precious things in his life.

But even that moment wasn't rock bottom. Not yet. Instead, Vaughn's death gave Johnson an excuse to drink and use drugs even more. He was sitting in a bar when he found out about Vaughn's death, and instead of going home, he finished off the bottle of Patron. He was so high at his son's funeral, he couldn't find the gravestone when he went back to the cemetery.

Anyone can understand the unspeakable pain a parent feels at the loss of a child. Vance blamed himself for not being there, for not being a better role model. He had been a Christian all his life, but in those dark, dark days he was convinced that God had turned away from him. "I still believed in God and I never blamed God, as many do; I just hid from Him in my sin."

> "Death didn't scare me. The next day never mattered anymore, the next drink or smoke did."

Vance rinsed and repeated with tequila and benzos until he stopped feeling any of the agonizing, crippling pain of that loss, numbing himself so much he ended up slipping into a coma that lasted twenty-eight days and nearly killed him. Even then, it wasn't enough to turn his life around. "Death didn't scare me. The next day never mattered anymore, the next drink or smoke did. I couldn't see past my own face."

It would be several months more before Vance finally said the words that would change his life: *Help me. I surrender.*

Two

Help

*"But whenever anyone turns to the Lord,
the veil is taken away."* – 2 Corinthians 3:16

It was the summer of 1972, and Trenton, New Jersey was hot and sticky, and the summer sun beat down on the pavement. Like most kids in the 70s, Vance and his cousins were outside from sunup to sundown, playing in the yard, shooting hoops at the playground down the street, and running races. Vance was a skinny kid and short compared to his older, taller cousins. Every summer, his parents made the trek from Tucson, AZ to Trenton to visit family for most of the season, which meant Vance spent plenty of hot summer days outside. His cousins dared him to race them down the street, with the winner getting a quarter. Vance raced everyone and anyone—family, strangers, kids he'd met in the park . . . if they challenged him, he ran.

Vance toed the line and when someone yelled "Go," he went. He was like a blaze of light down the street, hurtling past the other boys. He raced and he won—every single time. "I couldn't lose," he recalled. "I was lean and fast. I could catch a ball and I could run. It was during those summers that I realized I might have a gift—and that gift just might be my ticket out."

Tons of little boys dream of playing in the big leagues someday. They watch Kobe Bryant, Michael Jordan, Tom Brady, and dozens of other sports superstars living large, driving fancy cars and enjoying hordes of women and lavish parties. Only a fraction of kids make it to the pros. A 2013 survey by the NCAA laid out the reality of a young man's chances of making it to the NFL: Of the one million boys playing high school football today, only a third of them are still playing senior year. Of those 300,000 high school seniors, only 70,000 make it into the NCAA. Annually, a mere 6,500 players a year are scouted by the NFL, but only a handful—350—are invited to try out. About 300 make it, but only one hundred are still playing four years later.

> *Of the million boys putting on their shoulder pads and cleats, only .0001% make a career out of pro football.*

Think about it—of the million boys putting on their shoulder pads and cleats, only .0001% make a career out of pro football. To all of us on the outside looking in, these pro athletes seem to have it all. In reality, those careers rarely make the players rich. After taxes, the average player makes a little over a quarter million a year. Sure, that's a million dollars over four years, but if football is the only career you know and you're out of the game in your twenties, you'll have to budget to live off that million dollars for a very long time.

That's not what Vance was thinking about when he watched Franco Harris on the field with the Pittsburgh Steelers or Joe Namath playing for the Jets on Sundays. He wasn't doing the math or thinking about the statistics. He was picturing himself on that field, in a city far, far from the constant fights, and yelling, and beatings. "I tell people all the time, the only way I survived in the world I lived in was by making my own world in my head." When his father was drunk or hitting his mother, or the walls were shaking from arguments, Vance retreated to that space in his head where everything was wonderful because he had become something great. "In my mind I became a pro football player, an Olympian, or a professional runner."

He was gifted in all three sports and also in art. When he was seven, he was featured in the local paper for his art (his mom still has the clipping and proudly displays it). Instead of setting his sights on one goal, he concentrated on all of them at once. "They were all art, in a way. I would learn the sports and figure out what the penultimate step was, what my timing should be heading down the runway, where I should be on the field at any given time."

He repeatedly told himself that one of those options just had to work out and that would be his way out of the life he hated. He worked hard at everything he did, spending hours on the field or in the weight room. If his coach told him to run five miles, he ran five miles. If he was told to spend two hours in the weight room, he did. He worked harder and longer than anyone he knew, pouring every ounce of his energy into art and sports.

During track season, he used his speed in the 50-meter, 100-meter and 200-meter sprints, as well as in the 4x100-meter relay. But where Vance really shined was in long jump. He knew he didn't have a lot of upper body strength, so he concentrated on building his leg muscles. In 1982, at the age of seventeen, he won the NCAA long jump with a still-standing school record of 26 feet, 11 ¼ inches. That same year, he won a gold medal in the Junior Pan American games.

He placed second overall in the NCAA in 1983 and third in 1984, as well as third in that year's 4x100 relay.

Vance was so good that his college track coach told him he should try out for the 1984 Olympics. It was a three-day trial, held in Los Angeles. Vance nailed every single jump until the end. "I was on the team until the last jump, the last event that night. I see this other guy come on the field and hear everyone start clapping for him. He's running down the runway and...he beats me by less than an eighth of an inch, so I dropped down to an alternate." At the same time, Vance was looking at the NFL and knew he had to make a choice, because in the late 80s he couldn't be a professional in one sport and an amateur in another. He bowed out of the Olympics and set his sights on the NFL.

"I knew there were thousands of players who had the chance to go to the combine the year I went and only a certain number were drafted, but I was so sure I would be one of them," he recalled. Part of that came from his faith in God and his belief that his athletic ability was a sure sign of which direction he should go.

NFL scouts came to the University of Arizona (which Vance chose partly to be close to his mother because he worried about her and partly because it was Coach Brown's alma mater) and timed Vance in the 40-yard dash. He ran it in 4.28 seconds.

A time of 4.4 in the 40 is considered very fast, and when it was reported that Vance had shaved more than a tenth of a second off that time, reporters brought stopwatches the day Johnson was to be timed again in rookie camp. That time, he ran it in 4.36 seconds.

When the Broncos picked him in the draft and later offered him a little over a million dollars for four years, Vance said yes. Before he knew it, all that money would be gone, and he would be reduced to couch surfing because he had nowhere to live. But on that bright, sunny day when his name was called by the Denver Broncos, it seemed as if what everyone had said to him all his life was true—his athleticism was a gift from God and his life would be richly blessed for it.

"I was deceived from a young age, believing the gifts I had were to be used to make me happy." Vance grew up a Baptist but began following the Catholic tradition of crossing himself, and often pointed at the sky when things went well on the field. "I thought that was good enough, for people to see I was a believer."

With that NFL contract came houses, and cars, and anything and everything Vance could imagine. Just before the draft, his sports agent took him to a Porsche dealership in Arizona and urged him to buy a car to look the part, given how much money the speedy wide receiver would undoubtedly make. That day, Vance bought a Porsche 944. "That was kind of the beginning. I bought a boat, then a Ford F-150 just for pulling my boat to the lake. I bought a Porsche 911, a Ferrari 328, a Mercedes, then another Porsche—I had thirty cars during my career."

> *When his name was called by the Denver Broncos, it seemed as if what everyone had said to him all his life was true—his athleticism was a gift from God and his life would be richly blessed.*

Just like cars, he collected houses. Three in different parts of Colorado, some just because. "I bought a condo and only spent three nights there the entire time I owned it."

As fast as he made the money, Vance spent it, trying to fill the yawning cavern inside that grew wider and deeper by the second. The NFL was a non-stop party, but as he had with every single thing in his life, Vance took it up a notch. He essentially became the best at partying, the best at scoring women, the best at everything. Yet still it wasn't enough.

He conceived his first child, his daughter, just before college. His girlfriend's father told him to do the right thing and abandon football to marry his daughter. He even offered to get Vance a job as a firefighter. Vance refused and headed off to become an Arizona Wildcat. He'd sneak off campus from time to time to see his daughter.

While he was in college, his new girlfriend got pregnant and his first son was born. Around that time, the NFL called and Vance moved to Colorado. "When I stepped off the plane in Denver, I saw the newspaper headlines that said: *Broncos Add Vance*. I was happy. I had left hell and I had everything I wanted."

Underneath it all, Vance was still the shy kid who stuttered. So he affected a persona he nicknamed "The Vance". This version of Vance Johnson was strong, confident, charming with women, and unafraid in any social situation. Becoming that other person was his way of giving himself permission to do all the things he had avoided his entire life, like partying.

His dad came into town one night, and Vance took him out to a bar. Vance didn't want his father to know he had started drinking, so he had a soda. He talked to a girl at the bar, got her number, and put it on a cocktail napkin that accidentally got thrown away. The next day, Vance went back to the bar, dove into the dumpster and found the girl's number. They started dating, had sex, and a few months later she called him and announced she was pregnant. When she told him she was considering an abortion, Vance impetuously asked her to marry him. They got married in a Las Vegas drive-thru chapel for the bargain price of twelve dollars. Shortly after that, his son Vaughn was born.

Vance had finally settled down. He had a family, a house in Denver, and a garage filled with cars. One day, he was in the shower of the Broncos locker room and heard several other men mention his wife. They bragged about sleeping with her and Vance saw red. He ran home, and as soon as he got in the door he screamed at his wife. "I'd been drinking and I'd taken some pills. I was out of my mind. I ran upstairs and I was so mad, I pushed her across the bed and she hit her head. She stopped moving and I thought she was dead. I kept trying to wake her up, and when she didn't, I carried her into the bathroom and splashed water on her face until she came to."

Vance went back in the bathroom and looked at himself in the mirror. What he saw was the very man he had vowed he would never become—his father.

Vance went back in the bathroom and looked at himself in the mirror. What he saw was the very man he had vowed he would never become—his father. He had done all the things he swore he never would—drank, used drugs, and worst of all, hurt a woman. The level of shame and disappointment in himself was crushing, something he later confessed to Oprah Winfrey on her show. He never hurt a woman again—instead he got divorced at the first sign of an argument. But just like moving to Arizona as a kid, a change of marital status or a change of address didn't make anything different.

His life would get much, much worse before it got better. The crazy life that came with signing an NFL contract, coupled with pills and booze, caused him to spiral down into the depths of addiction and despair until he was homeless and stealing change from his friends to buy food. He'd wake up on someone's couch, scrounge together some quarters and dimes to grab a couple burritos at Taco Bell, then report to Mile High Stadium for practice. He'd have a car repo'd in the morning and by that afternoon be signing for another, because all anyone saw was Vance Johnson, NFL superstar.

"The Bible says that people are destroyed due to lack of knowledge (Hosea 4:6) and that 'There is a way that *appears* to be right, but in the end it leads to death.' (Proverbs 14:12). For a long time, I thought I took the path God wanted me to. I had this gift, and this career, and all this money . . . but I couldn't see that following my way, my rules, was also taking me straight down a road to dying."

Vance told himself he could have whatever he wanted. The rules didn't apply, not to him. That kind of mental justification led him down some crazy roads, including one where he kidnapped his own son from the mall one day. Vance and his ex-wife had been through an acrimonious divorce and Vance hadn't seen his son in quite some time. He happened to be in the same mall as his ex-wife and son, and saw his son shopping alone. "I saw him through the glass, so I went out to him and asked if he wanted to come with me. To hang out." Vance took his son home with him and called his ex-wife to tell her that he had the child. She had been frantic, and furious. In his head, Vance justified it—*I'm his father, so how's it wrong?*

The pills and alcohol whispered the same message— it's okay, it's not your fault.

The pills and alcohol whispered the same message—*it's okay, it's not your fault.* But when the substances wore off, Vance was left with crippling guilt and self-hatred. To quiet those feelings, he used more, and the vicious cycle only got worse and worse.

In the second step of recovery, one of the things addicts must do is realize that they can't recover on their own. That the way they've been doing things for months, years, sometimes decades, isn't going so well, and the only way back to sanity is by reaching out for help to a higher power. For Vance,

> *"God was always there, on the other side of the glass, waiting for me to turn to Him and go with Him."*

that higher power was always God. "For a long time I didn't believe I was worthy of being saved because I had destroyed so many lives, but God was bigger than my sins. I started to remember the broken in the Bible, like Jonah and King David, and I knew if He could help them, He could help me."

It wasn't until many years later, when he had gone through recovery and was speaking all over the country and telling his story, that Vance saw the irony in that moment in the mall with his son. "In my life before recovery, I was a child running around in the mall of life, buying everything I wanted, feeding my addictions, feeding my flesh and not really looking towards God. I was too distracted by all the things in front of me, but God was always there, on the other side of the glass, waiting for me to turn to Him and go with Him."

Three

Surrender

"Whoever wants to be my disciple must deny themselves and take up their cross and follow me. For whoever wants to save their life[a] will lose it, but whoever loses their life for me will find it. What good will it be for someone to gain the whole world, yet forfeit their soul? Or what can anyone give in exchange for their soul? – Matthew 16:24-26

That last line in Matthew 16:26 was something that resonated with Vance when he finally decided to get sober. He had the world at his feet—cars, boats, houses, women, NFL contracts, Super Bowl trips—but somewhere along the way, he lost his soul. He hurt almost everyone he knew. Ruined his relationships with his wives and children. Destroyed his friendships. He became someone he no longer recognized when he woke up in the morning. Rock bottom is about realizing that the personal price you pay for your

> *Rock bottom is about realizing that the personal price you pay for your addiction is far greater than the high you get from using.*

addiction is far greater than the high you get from using. But when Vance Johnson finally hit rock bottom, he wasn't so sure there was enough of his soul left to save.

Recovery from addiction is often likened to a journey because, like any trip from one point to another, there are good intentions when you set out, with inevitable detours and breakdowns along the way. That's pretty much how recovery went for Vance when he realized he needed to get it together or he was going to die.

The odds, however, were stacked against him, nearly as bad as his odds of making it into the NFL:

- According to the Centers for Disease Control, 114 people a day die from drug overdoses.

- Another 6,000-plus are sent to the ER on any given day.

- More than 90% of people who need rehab don't get treatment.

- Statistics claim there is a 30% success rate in rehab, but the reality is most addicts drop out of treatment at the three- to six-month mark, according to Joseph Califano, Jr., founder of the National Center on Addiction and Substance.

- According to *The New York Times,* state and federal governments spend an average of $15 billion on recovery services annually.

Despite the pressing need, the dollars spent on recovery and the number of centers or beds available, *up to 60% of addicts relapse after treatment,* according to the National Institute on Drug Abuse. Multiple agencies estimate that the relapse rate within the first thirty days is as high as 70%. Why? Partly simple math, both in numbers of people and in dollars and cents. The cost of recovery is high, not all insurance plans cover it, there are limited beds, and most addicts argue that they can't leave their jobs or family for that long. Long-term inpatient rehab has much higher success rates, but the reality is that few people can commit to or afford a residential program lasting three months or more.

And there's another factor, one that Vance discovered when he tried and failed to get sober on his own: A very small 1985 study published by *The Journal of Studies on Alcohol* found that alcoholics who were successful in rehabilitation had a multi-pronged approach that went beyond the 12-step program and a recovery center. These addicts had a combination of willpower, a physical aversion to alcohol after hitting rock bottom, and some kind of *life-changing experience*.

Vance's life-changing moment came at the bottom of a Colorado canyon in 2013. Several months earlier, Vance had come out of the coma and decided he would stay sober, but was determined to do it on his own. After all, thus far he had achieved everything he set out to do. Right? Surely staying sober would be just another goal to reach. Like he had when he'd trained for races and football games, he figured he would put his head down, work hard, and he'd succeed. Yeah, not so much this time.

People talk about quitting cold turkey, but the reality is that addiction isn't about willpower.

Vance lasted three or four months, and even then he wasn't 100% sober. He was still smoking weed to deal with his anxiety and urges to use, and had no real framework in place to support his recovery. He went to shoot a round of golf and figured he could have one Mike's Hard Lemonade. He spiraled out of control after that, dropping back into his world of pills and alcohol, abusing both more than ever before. People talk about quitting cold turkey, but the reality is that addiction isn't about willpower. If it were, every alcoholic, heroin addict, oxy user, and shopaholic, could potentially just decide to quit and they would be "cured".

The addiction is there for a reason. It has become that person's coping mechanism for life. Without a strong support system in place and a new set of coping skills, their recovery is doomed to fail. The overwhelming *I must have it, I can't live without it* feeling of any addiction is intensely powerful. In those first thirty days, and often throughout the first three months, most people in recovery are hanging on by a thread—minute-by-minute, sometimes second-by-second. That's why experts advise addicts to go to ninety meetings in ninety days—that urge to use is insanely strong, a daily reminder of why you need to stay on track is necessary.

For example, have you ever seen a smoker try to quit? Since 1970, there's been a giant warning label on every pack of cigarettes cautioning they could cause lung cancer and kill you. Cigarettes, and the nicotine in them, are the most commonly used and abused addictive substance in the United States; and they're legal. Almost a half a million people die each year from smoking-related illnesses. Yet, even with all the information, PSAs, doctor lectures, and warning labels, about 15% of Americans—a whopping 46 million people— continue to light up *every single day*. *US News and World Report* reported 95% of smokers who try to quit on their own go right back to smoking. Why? Because smoking is so ingrained in their daily life that it's almost like Jenga—pull the cigarettes out and the day threatens to crumble. Cigarettes are the first thing a smoker reaches for in the morning and the nicotine rush they turn to when they're stressed. It's the thing they use to socialize with smoking friends or hang out in their favorite bar—it's in every single inch of the fabric of the smoker's life. And on top of that, according to multiple sources (the *New York Times*, the Council on Chemical Abuse, etc.), nicotine is more addictive than heroin and the body craves what it has grown to rely upon.

That's what Vance faced—what any addict faces. His entire world centered around the pills and alcohol. While playing in the NFL, life was a constant party. After he left football, many of his friends still lived that lifestyle. His body had become so conditioned and reliant on alcohol and pills that he literally could not function without them. He didn't know how to quit, because he couldn't remember how to live without using.

> *Before the act of surrender and admitting the need for help, the addict has to realize that the only way out of this mess is by ceding control.*

Before the act of surrender and admitting the need for help, the addict has to realize that the only way out of this mess is by ceding control. For most people, handing over control of anything, even the TV remote, is counterintuitive. *I'm strong, I can do this, I can handle it on my own.* At one time or another, we all think that way. However, Vance was a man who was fast and powerful, cheered on by tens of thousands of people, so admitting he couldn't do this on his own and that he had lost control of himself, took far longer.

When Vance was a kid, he kept his world under tight control. His shoes were polished, his room tidy, and any speck of dirt was swept up right away. Things outside his control seemed to be in a constant state of chaos, nothing but arguments and fights, so Vance rigorously controlled everything he could. "I always did my homework, went to bed early, never snuck out, and didn't ditch school. I didn't get in trouble, didn't break any laws." When he was four or five years old, he stole candy from a store. His mother saw him and told the store owner to call the cops. The police showed up and scared little Vance straight by threatening to take him to jail. "I never stole anything again. I was a good kid."

He grew up watching his father lie about how much he drank and the other women he tried to hide. His life was a lie—the outside world believed everything at home was okay. Vance learned to keep his cards close to his vest and said nothing to his coaches or teachers about his home life. As a result, he lived his teenage years with rigid control and walked a straight and narrow line.

Then came the NFL, and with it the heady realization that he was *somebody*. There was a certain level of entitlement and untouchability that came with joining the Broncos. No longer just an ordinary kid, he was now Vance Johnson, superstar wide receiver. He was amazing on the field in his ten seasons with the Broncos. During Super Bowl XXI, he recorded five catches for 121 yards and scored a touchdown. At his peak in 1989, he made seventy-six receptions for a total of 1,095 yards and made seven touchdowns. Overall in his career, Vance had 415 receptions for 5,695 yards, made thirty-seven touchdowns, rushed seventeen times, gained 689 yards on punt returns, and 1,027 yards returning kickoffs.

"I did the right thing all the way to the NFL but when I got there, my thinking became warped. I was convinced that my way was the right way. After all, everything I had done brought me to the NFL, got me into the Super Bowl, so of course my way was correct. In my head, that gave me the right to do whatever I wanted to do. To drink hard and take pills. To not stay in my relationships. To get divorced over and over again. To drive a hundred miles an hour down the highway."

It was as if Vance had only read the first half of that verse from Proverbs 14:12. "There is a way that appears to be right…" It *all* seemed right. After all, hadn't his decisions brought him to football's biggest stage? "There was no one there to tell me I was wrong. There were articles about what I did— remember, there was no social media back then—and there were some consequences; I was embarrassed. But I was this famous pro football player now. So I didn't care."

> "I kept missing God. He was standing there on the other side of the glass, waiting for me to wake up to the truth."

In fact, the team, which was his only real boss during his time in the NFL, rarely disciplined him for anything he did. He literally had no one to answer to—except God—but Vance wasn't listening to what God had to say in those days. "I didn't know what type of person I was back then. I just thought I was right all the time because everything I wanted, I had. In Biblical terms, it talks about the lusts of the eye and being deceived. That was me. I was lusting after women, cars, houses, and thought they were all meant to be mine because of how hard I had worked. I was running around in that mall, getting everything I wanted, thinking I was a believer. But I kept missing God. He was standing there on the other side of the glass, waiting for me to wake up to the truth."

In the Merriam-Webster dictionary, there are four definitions for *surrender*: to yield to the power, control, or possession of another upon compulsion or demand; to give up completely or agree to forgo especially in favor of another; to give (oneself) up into the power of another; to give (oneself) over to something (such as an influence). But beneath all that, in small print, Merriam-Webster says the core definition of surrender is to yield.

Yield. To give up and cease resistance or contention. That's much easier said than done when you're a man used to being in control, who is so sure he's following the right path. A man who had virtually no consequences, as he said, and so he just kept the party going.

"The faster I went with partying, with women, with cars, the more I kept thinking I would find my joy. One time, I was driving to California from Colorado. I was on the highway, going 154 mph in one of my Porsches. I got pulled over by a cop in an airplane. He landed near me and was furious with me. He told me he's going to arrest me. I told him who I was and, just like that, the ticket was gone, and he's escorting me back to the state line."

Vance liked to gamble, too. One time he lost a considerable sum of money and the casino held him hostage until the Broncos paid his debt. The message there was clear—do what you want and it's totally cool. No one's going to fire you, arrest you, or give you any consequences. So, for almost three decades, that's exactly what he did.

At the same time, he was partying and hopping from one marriage to another, one woman to the next, he was desperately unhappy. Many times, he attempted suicide—his wrists still bear the scars of an unsuccessful attempt. Another time, his mother called just in time and told her son simply, "I was praying for you." It was enough for him to choose to live another day.

Over and over again, Vance's life was spared. Car accidents, speeding down slick roads on a motorcycle, overdoses on benzos and alcohol. None of it killed him—but it came close. After his NFL career ended, he ping-ponged between different businesses. Real estate, a trucking business with one of his wives, and then a string of restaurants in Colorado. He slept with the restaurant owner's niece and then proposed to her. At the same time, he started sleeping with another woman who worked at the same restaurant and proposed to her too. "I was so drunk and high I wasn't thinking straight. I sat the two of them down and said I had to choose between them. The two women were mad at me, but I said, 'I guarantee one of you will leave here as my wife.'" Maybe it was his cockiness or his natural charm, but the first woman did end up marrying him and became Mrs. Vance Johnson number six.

At the first sign of trouble, Vance bailed on the marriage, and quickly found wife number seven. But like every other relationship, every marriage, he cheated constantly. "I was sleeping with every woman I met. Women who worked in the restaurant, women I just met. I had sex in the kitchen, in the walk-in fridge, in the bar. I was deep in the dirt but I couldn't see it."

His parents moved in with him and took over the day-to-day operations because he was too drunk and high to run the restaurants, which were rapidly failing. "I moved into a home I rented from a friend back in Parachute, near the restaurant, with my dog Munch. She was a bulldog and my only companion. I would show up at the restaurant only to be told by my mom to go home. Instead of leaving, I'd sneak through the back, go downstairs, and break into the liquor storage room. My mom put a key lock on the door, but I always figured out a way to get in. Sometimes she'd find me out back, puking blood, drunk. She had the saddest look on her face (even thinking about that look now fills me with regret). She would say, 'Son, please go get some rest.' But we both knew sleep wasn't what I needed."

Vance met another woman online and got married to her—without remembering to divorce his seventh wife first. His life had spun so far out of control he couldn't find so much as a string to pull it back together. When he went to sleep at night, he'd have so many bottles beside him that he couldn't tell which was which. He was often too wasted to go to the bathroom, so he'd use an empty bottle, then forget that he'd peed in that bottle until he went to take a drink. The pills knocked him out so deeply, sometimes he couldn't even make it from the bathroom to his bed and would pass out on the floor. In those days, he couldn't tell people what day it was, what year it was, or even who he was. He'd fallen so far down the rabbit hole that he didn't know which way was up.

"One night, I called my mom and said, 'I'm gonna die.' I was vomiting and peeing blood. When my mother got there, she said I was turning blue. She took me to the hospital, and I went into a coma that night."

> *His life had spun so far out of control he couldn't find so much as a string to pull it back together.*

Twenty-eight days later, Vance woke up and found himself chained to the bed because he'd tried to pull his IVs and catheter out. "Here I am, lying in this bed, crapping all over myself. The nurses would have to come in, roll me over, and wipe me off. I'm fifty years old. I was in the NFL. I played in the Super Bowl. And I couldn't even get to the bathroom on my own anymore." His life had fallen to an all-new low he could barely comprehend.

Even he didn't know how close he'd been to dying until just a few months ago. He was talking to his mother on the phone and she told him that the hospital had her call and tell his sister and his oldest daughter they needed to come. They were his next of kin, and Vance was so far gone the doctors asked his daughter to make the decision whether or not they should turn off the machines. She called her siblings, and together they decided their father wouldn't want to live like that. So, when she went back to the hospital, she signed a form giving them permission to unhook him from life support. "They were waiting for me to die. I didn't know it got that bad or went that far."

While Vance was in the coma, he remembers hearing people talking to him. He started seeing shadows walking into his room every day, shadows of different heights and sizes. The shadows would look at him and leave. He had an out-of-body experience where he floated to different floors in the hospital and tried to talk to people, but they wouldn't or couldn't talk back. Later, when he told his nurses and doctors about the experience, they agreed they had been in those rooms and on those floors, but Vance wasn't there.

His hospital room had a view, and he remembers turning to look at the sky, a helpless man now who could no longer get to the bathroom on his own, and thinking, *Really God? Is this where I'm going to end up?*

When the hospital released him, Vance's parents took him into their own home and helped him, literally, get back on his feet. He'd barely escaped death, and he knew the alcohol and pills were to blame. "I decided to stay sober. I prayed a lot and worked out all the time. Then I went golfing, had a drink, and it all went downhill from there."

His seventh ex-wife saw the condition Vance was in and called Randy Grimes, a former Tampa Bay Buccaneer who had been sober for many years. She begged him to contact Vance. She told Grimes her ex-husband was killing himself. Randy called Vance and they talked many, many times, but every time, Vance lied to him. *I'm fine. I have it under control.*

Then one day, he was driving from Parachute to Grand Junction, winding his way through the deep, picturesque canyons of Colorado. His life had become a living hell and, no matter what he did, he couldn't seem to escape the insanity. "The only thing lower than me was a river that I wanted to drive into. I started screaming out to God, begging Him to help me. I started speaking in tongues, the words coming from my mouth were a gibberish I didn't understand. I just kept screaming and begging Him for help."

Vance kept crying out and begging God for help, day and night, for weeks on end. He screamed into an empty space, over and over. And then one night, he heard a whisper from the Lord—Vance needed to go be alone with Him. "I woke up in the morning and told Randy I was ready to go. Randy said, 'Let's get you on a plane now.'"

But it was a Friday and Vance still couldn't quite let go, couldn't quite yield yet. He looked at all the bottles of tequila and vodka in his room—the friends he had relied on for so long—and he replied, "I'll go Monday." He drank the rest of his stash but kept his promise on Monday morning and got on the plane to a recovery center in Florida.

> *His life had become a living hell and, no matter what he did, he couldn't seem to escape the insanity.*

He thought that would be the end of his difficult road, but the hard part was still to come.

Four

Examine

Search me, God, and know my heart; test me and know my anxious thoughts. See if there is any offensive way in me and lead me in the way everlasting. – Psalms 139:23-24.

Let us examine our ways and test them, and let us return to the Lord. – Lamentations 3:40

As the plane lifted off from Denver International Airport that Monday morning in November 2013, Vance snapped a picture of the city he was leaving. "I knew at that moment that things were going to be different. *I* was going to be different. I wasn't coming back to the same place. I wasn't, in fact, coming back to anything."

He had no wife, no family, no house, no possessions, no restaurant, and no parents to return to because he had burned every single bridge with them. He'd hurt people, rejected their help, ignored their advice; acted out and acted up. He'd lost every

> "I wasn't coming back to the same place. I wasn't, in fact, coming back to anything."

dime he had, at that time was over a million dollars in debt, two of his three restaurants had gone belly up, and he'd lost control of the third one when his parents came in and took over Vance Johnson's Outlaw Ribbs. He'd even pawned the Super Bowl rings he worked so hard to achieve. He was too poor to afford rehab, which thankfully was being covered by the NFL Cares fund. At that moment, Vance Johnson had, quite literally, nothing.

"And yet I was so happy to be going to treatment. I told everyone around me where I was headed." He hadn't used alcohol in a couple of days but had yet to give up the pills. He imagined the Florida rehab facility to be basically a no-alcohol party with hot girls on the beach playing volleyball. He had a rude awakening when he checked in for his twenty-eight-day stay.

"I was strip searched right after intake. I'd never gone through anything like that before." The treatment center wanted to make sure he wasn't smuggling in any pills or alcohol and searched his bags and his body. The detox caused dangerously high blood pressure (as high as 220/160), so the center worried he might have a stroke. They took his vitals every fifteen minutes until they could get it regulated. The immediate invasion of privacy was unsettling and he had difficulty acclimating.

His roommate was another pro ball player, a man in similar circumstances, but Vance didn't see him that way at first. "Right away, I started judging him. Here I am trying to get clean, but the old me is still there judging everyone I meet."

There were, of course, no volleyball nets on the beach, no girls in bikinis, and no parties with virgin piña coladas. Instead, there were meetings and therapy and hard questions. For the first few days, Vance rebelled against the process.

The center, which operated on the principles of Alcoholics Anonymous, adhered to the message of relying on "the God of your understanding". The first time Vance heard that, he leapt to his feet and yelled at the leader, saying there was no God but *the* God. One of the behavioral health technicians told him he needed to sit down and listen or he'd be kicked out. Vance sat down, but he didn't listen.

He looked around the room and saw men of all ages and from all backgrounds. There was a handful of professional athletes. In his eyes, they were all different from him. "All I saw was a bunch of crack addicts and alcoholics. I thought, *that's not me. I'm an NFL player. I'm not one of these people.*"

He withdrew from the activities, refused to share in group, and kept to himself. He argued against the rules and the curfew. Every day, he walked the perimeter of the property, staying just inside the fence. Across the street from the center was a church with a cross on top of the building. "One day, I walked all the way to the front gate. I looked at that gate and thought about leaving. Then I saw that cross and I heard a voice inside me say 'go back inside because you are sick and this is where you need to be'. Later on, I realized it was the Holy Spirit keeping me where I needed to be."

> *Outsiders might think the lessons and tools are the keys to recovery, but the biggest secret to successful recovery from any addiction is listening.*

Vance did go back inside and brought a new attitude with him. He asked for a recovery Bible and began to read it and pray more regularly. He sat down in group, and instead of sitting there thinking that he wasn't like these other men, he decided to listen.

Outsiders might think the lessons and tools are the keys to recovery, but the biggest secret to successful recovery from *any* addiction is listening. Active listening—without judgement—means the person is no longer listening to, and focusing on, only themselves. A person engages and listens to and draws lessons from other people who have been there, done that, and survived to tell the tale. Active listening allows the addict to not only hear success stories, but the stories of failure, and learn from other people's choices and setbacks. When Vance stopped listening to his inner desires for women, pills, and alcohol, and started listening to other people who had traveled the same road of trauma and addiction, he not only learned he wasn't alone but was able to open his heart and be willing to listen to the voice of God.

"I was surrounded by these guys in their twenties, thirties, and forties. They were talking about how they had been abused as children, how they got hooked on pornography or pills or alcohol, how they were traumatized in their lives, and I realized I was listening to *my* story. I stopped judging them and saw them as people just like me."

But he wasn't quite ready to join in and share his own history. In his head, he was still Vance Johnson, gold medalist at the Pan American games in long jump and retired NFL player who'd made it to the Super Bowl three times. He joined a small private group of professional athletes and discovered some commonalities among their differences. Many of the football players suffered from Post-Concussion Syndrome (PCS), which has been linked to Chronic Traumatic Encephalopathy (CTE). The repeated head trauma football players suffer on the field causes impulse control problems, memory lapses, depression, paranoia, and aggression.

CTE is becoming a major issue in the NFL. Of the 111 brains of deceased former football players donated to science and studied for this disease, 99% of them (110) had signs of CTE. About 250 concussions per year are diagnosed by NFL doctors, but estimates of the number of unreported concussions are much, much higher. The American Academy of Neurology released a study in 2016 that estimated more than 40% of former NFL players show signs of traumatic brain injuries. While the link between brain injuries and addiction is difficult to establish (because there are so many factors that go into addictive behaviors), in July 2009, the *Journal of Neurotrauma* published research that supports the theory that the cognitive deficits caused by repeated injuries to the brain can lead to substance abuse problems or prohibit those already addicted to become drug or alcohol free—it's a vicious cycle.

Like many players, Vance suffered several concussions during his ten years in the NFL. "I was a little guy and I got hit a lot. When you hit the ground that hard, it feels like your brain is shaking inside your skull." When a player was disoriented or confused after his head slammed into the ground or there was helmet-to-helmet contact, the team doctor ran onto the field and performed an on-the-spot neurological check. "But we didn't want to quit playing or lose a crucial guy in the middle of a game. So other guys come up behind the guy with a concussion and helped him. When the doctor said, "Don't look up, tell me the score," there was always another teammate behind us whispering, "It's 14 to 7." If the doctor asked me to point out which sideline was mine, one of my teammates would nudge me on the right or left side. There were times when I was hit so hard, I couldn't remember what quarter it was or what play we were running. The other guys would say, "Just take off and run down the field. We've got you.""

Since he left the NFL, Vance has gone in for baseline testing to see if he shows signs of having suffered a traumatic brain injury. The results were inconclusive, but the doctors aren't ready to say he doesn't have a TBI and are still evaluating him.

The other thing Vance noticed among the "famous" residents at the treatment center was a reluctance to dive deep. Like the concussion coverups on the field, professional athletes are used to saying they're fine when they really aren't fine at all. "Much of what the other pros talked about was very shallow." Vance understood that because he also struggled with admitting his history and acknowledging he was just like all the other "ordinary" people in treatment. Finally making that connection and getting real with the other men in the program was the breakthrough that Vance needed.

He started participating in group. He finally shared his history with his father with his therapist, as well as the devastating loss of his son. He began going to art and music therapy classes and attended both Narcotics Anonymous and Alcoholics Anonymous meetings. Every Sunday, he got on the bus to go to church. In between, he read his Bible and got on his knees and talked to God. "That first Sunday I went to church, I sat close to the front. As the pastor started to speak, I realized it was the first time I'd been sober in church since

Like the concussion coverups on the field, professional athletes are used to saying they're fine when they really aren't fine at all.

I was a little boy. This time, I was clean and I could hear the message. For too many years, I'd show up in church as "Vance Johnson" and make sure to put my money in the plate while people were watching to prove I was a believer. Now I was here, listening to the preacher as just a man trying to get closer to the Lord."

Day by day, Vance opened up more and began to look at the disaster his life had become. The more he did, the harder it got, and his journey became increasingly painful. The hardest day of all, the one that still makes him choke up and brings tears to his eyes, was the day his therapist had him hold a mock funeral for his son.

When Vaughn died, Vance got drunk and high before the funeral and stayed that way for many years after. It wasn't just about his grief—it was about the crushing guilt. The day Vaughn died, he'd called his dad and asked him to help pay for a new engine for Vaughn's car, which was in the shop. Vance—too busy and too self-involved—said no, and told Vaughn to get a job and work for the money to pay for the engine. Vaughn couldn't afford it, so he got a motorcycle instead—the very motorcycle he was riding when the SUV plowed into him and killed him. "I can't blame God for my son's death. It was my fault. I wasn't there when he needed me. I was never there when he needed me."

A fellow resident at treatment confronted him and asked him if he had celebrated all the events in his life: weddings, birthdays, game wins, time spent out with the guys. "Of course," Vance replied.

"And you celebrated your son's death?" the other man enquired.

Immediately, Vance became furious and said there was no way he had celebrated that horrific event. The other man asked a different question. "Did you drink and do drugs after your son died?" When Vance nodded and the other man shrugged. "Then you celebrated that the same way you celebrated everything else."

Back in his room, Vance realized that he had, indeed, treated the death of his son the same as every other event in his life—non-stop binging on drinks and pills. He didn't deal with his emotions. He never bothered to give himself time to acknowledge or process his feelings. Treatment, however, didn't allow him those crutches and he was going to have to ride out and work through his pain.

Vance stood in front of the group while another man lay on the floor at his feet, eyes closed, playing the part of Vaughn, Vance's deceased son. "I stood over him and said all the things I should have said to Vaughn but couldn't because I was too high to speak at his funeral. How sorry I was. That I felt like it was my fault he was dead. How much I loved him. I talked about how proud I was of him as a child, and as an adult. How much I wished I had been in his life and been there for him."

When Vance was done, his therapist said, "Now, switch places and be your son. Tell yourself what you think he would say to you."

Vance lay down on the cold, impersonal tile floor and crossed his arms over his chest. He closed his eyes and laid there for a moment, thinking of Vaughn, of how short his son's life had been, and how his little boy was lying in the ground somewhere, cold and gone. The guilt Vance had carried inside for six long years poured out of him. "I looked up at the other man, who was playing me, and I said, 'Dad, I'm so disappointed in you. You were my hero and now look what you're doing to yourself. I'm so ashamed of you. I can't believe all the things you've done in your life, all the choices that led you to this moment. You're worthless to everyone and you're killing yourself. I died because of you.'"

The therapist told Vance to get to his feet and switch places one more time. It was now time to tell his son what he felt about the words he had just said. The other man lay on the tile again, and Vance looked down at him, sobbing while trying to get the words out, words he hadn't ever been able to say. "All I could say was, 'I'm so sorry, I love you so much, I'm not going to let this thing beat me. I'm going to be strong and make you proud. Because of you, I will try to save every young man I can, every young man who had a father like me. I am doing it for you, Vaughn, because you're my why.'"

His *why*. Every recovering addict needs a reason to stay sober, something to hold onto more precious and more important than their substance of choice. For Vance Johnson, his why was simple—the little boy he loved so much. Vaughn was the one person Vance would never have an opportunity to talk to and never be able to make amends with for the past.

"If I looked at my life—married and divorced eight times, in debt for a million dollars, homeless, alone, out of a job—I had no reason to get clean. No reason to want to stay sober. But that day, I realized I had a purpose. Vaughn—he was my reason—and God put me there so I could see that and use it to fuel the days ahead. I had such an important reason to stay sober and to help other people do the same."

> *"Because of you, I will try to save every young man I can, every young man who had a father like me. I am doing it for you, Vaughn, because you're my why."*

As he neared day twenty-eight—the day when he would have to go home and do this on his own—Vance got nervous. Inside the treatment center, staying sober was easy. He had no access to pills or alcohol. There were dozens of other things to do, places to go, people to talk to when the urge to use arose. At home, none of those things existed. The closest meeting was fifty miles away, and the people who had once been around him were gone. "I saw guys getting coined out (getting their thirty-day chip) and knew I had a long way to go yet. The demons I left behind were waiting for me. In the Bible, it says the demons go to the dry places and then they come back to see if the house—your mind and body—is empty so they can move back in. I needed to make sure my house was strong and able to withstand those demons."

"I had to be completely broken before I was ready for what God intended."

As a child and young man, Vance actualized every dream and goal he set for himself. Until it all began to crumble. He made—and lost—millions of dollars. He travelled all over the world, was once celebrated and adored, and literally had everything he ever wanted before it was all taken away from him. "The whole reason I achieved all of that was because I had to reach those heights and then be brought down so, so low. I had to be completely broken before I was ready for what God intended."

What that was, Vance wasn't quite sure. As he got on the plane that would take him back to Denver and all the temptations waiting for him there, he prayed for the strength and wisdom to be the kind of man who could finally make his son proud. This time he didn't need to take pictures. He had a vision of where he was going, and held tight to that as the plane taxied away from the place that had saved him.

Five

Confess

Therefore confess your sins to each other and pray for each other so that you may be healed. – James 5:16

Eighty thousand people watched the AFC Championship game in the 1986 season, when the Broncos played the Cleveland Browns. Number 82, Vance Johnson, was on the field, doing what he did best—catching the ball and running like hell down the field. In the fourth quarter, with five minutes and change to go, the Broncos were down, 20–13. Quarterback John Elway threw the ball to Vance, but the pass was incomplete. Undaunted, the Broncos kept at it, whittling away Cleveland's yardage more and more every second.

In those few minutes, Elway pulled off what has been referred to ever since (and in the movie *Hot Tub Time Machine*) as "The Drive", making fifteen plays that marched the Broncos ninety-eight yards down the field and they scored a touchdown in the last minute of the game. "My job in those last five minutes was to run down the middle of the field because I was being double teamed. In the huddle, Elway told me to do that so I could clear out the middle of the field. That gave everyone else a chance to catch the ball, and if he didn't throw it, he would run it for the first down." Vance was twenty-three years old, in his first AFC Championship game, and about to witness a miracle.

With the extra point a few seconds later, the fourth quarter ended in a tie. In overtime, the Broncos scored a field goal, beating the Browns 23-20 and sending the Denver team to the Super Bowl for the first time since 1977.

> *When his plane touched down at Denver International Airport almost three decades after that AFC win, there was no parade, no champagne, and no fans wearing a number 82 jersey.*

While the Broncos were busy on the field making history with those ninety-eight yards, the behind-the-scenes crew was busy taping plastic tarps over the locker room, readying dozens of bottles of champagne, and transforming the entire space into a party. All the way from the field, through the tunnel, and into the locker room, there were celebrations for the team—champagne sprays, Gatorade dumps, cheering fans. The blood of Broncos' fans runs orange, white, and blue, and they celebrated every single one of their boys on the field. That was the kind of reception Vance Johnson was used to—confetti, cheers, and adulation.

When his plane touched down at Denver International Airport almost three decades after that AFC win, there was no parade, no champagne, and no fans wearing a number 82 jersey. After his month in rehab, Vance returned an ordinary man with extraordinary problems.

He took a taxi back to a home that wasn't his. The debt created by his bad decisions lost him fourteen homes and two restaurants to foreclosure. At the age of forty-nine, the celebrated athlete was living with his parents. His credit was ruined. All his cars, houses, and fans were long gone. He returned, essentially, to the life he'd been so eager to leave as a little boy.

The months living at home were humbling and reminded him how far he had fallen from the glory days. "Since I'd left treatment and surrendered myself to God, I was okay not having anything. But it was really tough to face that reality at home and sober. I realized I had never had a moment before when I couldn't make something go away that I didn't want to hear or see or face. Now, all of that was right in front of me and I had to deal with it."

He had difficult, stressful meetings with his accountant, his friends, and his parents. His vision of being a retired athlete with a string of restaurants was not going to happen. He bought the restaurant that would become Vance Johnson's Outlaw Ribs first in 2007. He was at the height of his addiction then and everything went downhill when Vaughn died. His parents took over the restaurant and kicked Vance out. He opened Epicurious forty-five miles away, then opened VJ's Outlaw Ribbs, but none of the restaurants succeeded. "I was always drunk, in another marriage that was failing, and having multiple affairs. I was stealing food from Outlaw Ribbs to sell at Epicurious. It got to a point where I had to eventually shut the restaurant down and missed paying employees the last week. My reputation went to hell." The employees and patrons found out about the shutdown from a hand-written note left on the front door.

Vance later did a TV interview apologizing for not paying the workers and for shutting his doors so abruptly. He had a beautiful house in the Redlands with his wife, but he ended up kicking her and the kids out so he could keep on partying. "I partied a lot in downtown Grand Junction and many times would be too drunk to drive home. The norm for my life became blackouts, then waking up and having no clue where I was or where I lived. Between the anti-depressants, alcohol, pain killers, and smoking weed, I was barely navigating life. I had no idea what day of the week it was, what month, where I was going, and that made it incredibly difficult to even think about stopping. On top of that, being famous gave me no accountability."

After he came home from treatment, he faced critics who didn't believe he would really stay sober, and "friends" who wanted their party pal back. Pre-rehab Vance hosted barbecues and poker games that often went all night. He was always ready to knock back a few beers with some fans or hang out in the bar and tell stories of his glory days. But post-rehab Vance did none of those things. He tried going back to work at the restaurant, but the patrons who came into Vance Johnson's Outlaw Ribs weren't interested in the sober Vance. They wanted the ready-to-party guy they remembered. "Our bartender had quit so I took over behind the bar. I'd give fans a round of shots and they'd keep trying to get me to take one with them. When I didn't, they were disappointed, and sometimes they were mad."

The shy Vance who had been hidden behind the alcohol and pills returned, and he became withdrawn and quiet. Eventually, the fans who came to the restaurant to see "the Vance" stopped coming, and Vance's parents told him to stay home because his presence was making business worse instead of better. "I was fired from my own restaurant. I understood it because I was bad for business. People thought I was standoffish or arrogant, and they didn't understand why I didn't want to party."

Vance spent his days reading, praying, or sleeping, and not doing much else. "I had a lot of dead space in my life. I had nothing to do. I wasn't going to the restaurant, I wasn't hanging out with my friends. I spent a lot of time reading the Bible and going to church." He was incredibly lonely. The players he'd spent a decade with were still living the party life. The women he had hurt wanted nothing to do with him. His children, who hadn't had much of a relationship with him when he was using, had stopped talking to him. There was a hole in his life that he hadn't anticipated when he got sober. When he removed substance abuse from his life, he also removed the people, places, and things that went along with the lifestyle.

A 2017 article in *US News & World Report* stated most recovery programs recommend people don't get into relationships for at least a year after getting sober. There are several reasons behind this thinking: The road to recovery can be up and down in the months after sobriety; it's very easy and very common to replace one addiction with another (like a love addiction); people justify skipping their meetings or doing their step work because they want to spend time with their new love interest; and most of all, because a relationship is yet another distraction that gives the addict a new excuse to not focus on his issues and fears.

> *When he removed substance abuse from his life, he also removed the people, places, and things that went along with the lifestyle.*

For a man who had literally never lived alone, this guideline was the hardest for him to adhere to. Women pursued him just as they had when he was in the NFL, and it was hard to say no to their invitations.

He texted with a few women, talked to some others, and then started to date. One night, Vance didn't want to tell the woman he was with that he was a recovering addict. Maybe he was tired of telling the story, maybe he wanted to test himself—or maybe he just wanted to be quote-unquote normal—but when she offered him a glass of wine, he said nothing and drank it. "The alcohol did nothing for me but leave me with a lot of shame. I'd worked so hard, and here I was throwing that away. It was only the one glass and I never had another, but I call that a relapse because I took my eye off what was important for a moment. It was enough to convince me to never, ever, do that again." He even dated a woman after that who owned a bar and helped her carry in the boxes of liquor once in a while. Renewed in his commitment and reliant on his Bible and constant prayer, Vance has never been tempted to drink again.

He dated a little, having what he called "pass-through relationships", but none of them had any staying power. He knew he needed to concentrate on himself and, if he deviated from that course, it would be all too easy to end up back where he started. "I was in church one time with a woman I was dating, and the pastor made a comment about relationships outside of wedlock. I looked at her and said, 'This won't work.' I knew that wasn't what God wanted for me, but it was hard to be alone, too."

Four months after treatment, February 2014, he was invited to Super Bowl XLVIII played at the Meadowlands. It was the first Super Bowl for Peyton Manning, who was the quarterback for the Broncos, facing off against the Seattle Seahawks. "I went on fifty different radio and television stations to talk about professional athletes and addiction. Randy Grimes was there, and he had over five years clean then. The interviewer would talk to Randy and then turn to me. When I told them that I was four months clean, a lot of them didn't want to talk to me. 'You don't have any clean time,' they complained. I was so mad at that, and didn't understand why they didn't think I would stay sober."

Psychology Today published the results of an eight-year study of recovering alcoholics. Of the twelve-hundred people in the study, only a third of those with less than a year of sobriety stayed sober. For those with a year of sobriety, half relapsed. It was only with longer terms of sobriety that the relapse rates went down significantly. Out of the

> *Far too many athletes (and others) before Vance fell off the wagon early into their sobriety, and very few people believed in his commitment to staying away from the pills and alcohol.*

people with five years of sobriety, only 15% relapsed. "Four months is really young in your sobriety, especially being a former athlete. There's nothing except triggers waiting for you when you get out of treatment," Vance commented. The radio stations had seen this all before and didn't want to interview him about his success with sobriety only to see him in the papers a week later, falling back to his old ways. Far too many athletes (and others) before Vance fell off the wagon early into their sobriety, and very few people believed in his commitment to staying away from the pills and alcohol.

"I was disappointed that no one trusted I would stay clean. People didn't know how strong my faith was, and maybe that's because I'd only talked about God a little bit—not like I do now. I knew in my heart who I was in my walk, but it was going to take time for other people to know and believe that, too."

Gradually, he resumed living his life, returning to the restaurant for a while, heading to Christian meetings, and going on religious retreats. He drove all the way to Denver to go to church, building a new group of friends and support system. All the while, he was learning about recovery and immersing himself in the Bible because that, he knew, would illuminate the path forward. "I got on my knees every time I struggled or wanted to pick up a drink. There were so many times I wanted to, but I got on my knees and begged God. The only thing I could use was my Bible and my voice to cry out to God."

Real life kept intruding—things like child support, debts, and day-to-day bills meant Vance needed a job. Epicurious closed before he went to treatment, but Outlaw Ribbs in Parachute was hobbling along, close to being sold, and his NFL money dried up long ago. His parents struggled to keep the Parachute location open—his mother emptied her retirement account to pay the bills—but eventually it too would close its doors for good.

Vance had no job, no income stream, no prospects—and a hell of a lot of debt to pay off. He prayed for something to come his way, and nine months after he got home from Florida, the CEO of the treatment center called him up and asked Vance if he'd like to come work for them. They flew him back to Florida, put him up in a nice hotel, and had him come in for an interview.

"The day before, I'm thinking about what kind of salary I'm going to ask for. I was used to making $250-700,000 a year playing football, so I figured I'd take $150,000 a year. I went in there, talked to the CEO, and he said he wanted to hire me." Vance sat back in his chair, prepared to negotiate.

"I'll offer you fifteen," the CEO said.

"Fifteen what?" Vance enquired. "Fifteen thousand a month?"

The CEO leaned forward, his face serious, and replied, "Fifteen dollars an hour. Part-time. Twenty hours a week."

Vance sat there, stunned. Fifteen dollars an hour, at twenty hours a week, was $240 a week after taxes. He had gone from making more than a half a million dollars a year to a salary of just over $12,000 a year. "Where will I live? How will I get to work?"

"We'll toss in a bus pass, and we have some old houses that used to be part of our center down the street. We can let you live in one of those."

Relegated to riding a bus. Reduced to living in a rundown house no bigger than a trailer. Earning only two percent of the money he used to make. Vance shook the other man's hand and said he'd think about it. "On the way back to the airport, I called my mom. She said, 'The Lord will tell you what to do. I love you.' Then she hung up."

Back in Colorado, while he was still thinking about whether to accept the treatment center's job offer, Vance received an email from the Broncos. They offered him two thousand dollars a week to travel the country, show up at community events, and do nothing more than "be Vance Johnson".

Two thousand a week for being his former self versus two hundred and forty a week to work hard. The decision seemed like a no-brainer, but he struggled with the temptation of being back in his old life, no matter what they paid him. Vance called the treatment center on Friday and asked the CEO how long he had to make a decision. The CEO told him to take his time, that there was no rush.

> *The decision seemed like a no-brainer, but he struggled with the temptation of being back in his old life, no matter what they paid him.*

Vance took a long walk after that phone call, praying for the right answer. The lure of being part of the NFL again was strong, and Vance began to justify all the reasons why the offer from the Broncos would be too good to pass up. He figured he could work for the Broncos for three months, put some money in the bank, then go work at the treatment center. "But as I rounded the corner, I heard in my head, *Your flight leaves Monday*. I knew that was the Holy Spirit, telling me what to do. Which choice to make."

Nine months earlier, Vance had called Randy Grimes and said he was ready to go to treatment. It was a Friday, and Vance held onto his old friend's liquor and pills for a couple more days, leaving for the place that would change his life on a Monday.

After that fateful walk, ironically on another Monday, Vance booked himself a flight, packed a backpack of belongings, and got on a plane to Florida. He'd made up his mind and took the job that paid almost nothing but would come to mean almost everything.

When he got there, he was worried about how he could talk to the other guys and work with them. He had no training in mental health and only had ten months of sobriety. The treatment center, however, had seen something in Vance. He exhibited a realness, an openness, and had a way of connecting with other people and they knew the position would be a good fit, both for him and for the patients. "But how do I do that?" Vance worried.

The CEO looked at him, and simply replied, "Just be Vance Johnson."

Six

Cleanse

Humble yourselves before the Lord,
and He will lift you up. —James 4:10

For the first time in his life, Vance Johnson was happy. Broke as hell, living utterly alone, holding onto a bus pass for dear life, but happy. Truly, honestly, all the way to his toes happy. "Nobody wanted me, nobody cared about me, and I didn't owe anybody anything because I didn't have anything. Yet I was filled with so much joy."

Five days a week, Vance would leave his little one-bedroom "condo", then walk down an alley that led to the bus stop. He'd swipe his bus pass, ride to work, spend a few hours at the center, and then take the bus back. If he was late, he had to walk to work, no matter the weather. He was so used to a celebrity's lifestyle he had no idea the bus wouldn't wait for him if he wasn't on time. "I'd end up walking in the rain many times,

> *"I couldn't understand why I was so full for the first time in my life when I was so empty of possessions and people."*

but it was okay because I could smell the flowers and see the clouds. I would look up to the sky and say, 'God, thank you so much, I'm so happy.' I couldn't understand why I was so full for the first time in my life when I was so empty of possessions and people. I hadn't been that happy when I was sitting in a house with ninety-six windows, a Playmate on my couch, and a Porsche in the driveway. But here, with nothing, I was truly happy."

Two hundred and forty dollars a week doesn't go far, not even with a bus pass and free housing. The man who used to negotiate multi-million-dollar football contracts and buy multiple Porsches now negotiated to eat one meal a day at the treatment center so he could afford to buy himself dinner every day at a fast-food Mexican restaurant for four dollars and fifty-seven cents. "I had to go shopping for clothes with my first check, but to get to Walmart, I had to take the bus and take a transfer. I had no idea what a transfer was and had to ask people for help. I remember buying a three-dollar T-shirt, nine-dollar jeans, seven-dollar shoes, and then a couple pairs of socks for three dollars. I'm riding back home on the bus with my bag, and thinking my life is so good."

He lived in a thirty-four-room complex alone and swore he heard noises in the night and bumps against the wall. Whatever was causing the noises, Vance looked at them as one more challenge in his spiritual battle for his new life. If it was the Devil trying to scare him or to remind him how alone he was, Vance was determined to pray and keep his focus on God and what was important. In those months, getting himself back on track, no matter what it took, was what mattered. So he got up in the morning, put on his jeans and T-shirt, caught the bus, and then worked as many hours as the center would allow.

It was a step down, to be sure. He had been hired at the center to be, essentially, a ball boy. "I left being famous, being 'Vance Johnson' behind. Everyone in the state of Colorado knew who I was. When I met people, I shook hands, kissed babies... and then I got on a plane and flew across the country to be a ball boy in Florida. They gave me a key to the rec room so I could hand out volleyballs and basketballs. That was my job."

> *Humility allows the addict to see himself or herself more clearly, because it removes the fame, the bravado, and the self-aggrandizement, that allowed them to justify their behavior.*

It was the perfect job at the perfect time for him in his recovery. Step six is about being humble. Experts say that without this part of recovery addicts may stay sober, but they will be bitter and resentful and blame others. The addict has admitted their weakness and their need for help. They've looked at their past behavior and shortcomings. They have seen the damage they left in their wake when they let substances become more important than job, friends, and family. But many get stuck in that spot because moving forward to things like amends requires humbling yourself. Humility allows the addict to see himself or herself more clearly, because it removes the fame, the bravado, and the self-aggrandizement, that allowed them to justify their behavior.

Luke 8:5-6 tells a story about a farmer sowing seeds. He didn't watch where he was dropping them and "some fell on rocky ground, and when it came up, the plants withered because they had no moisture." The rocks, essentially, prevented the seeds from growing. In recovery, there's a similar parable that is used to teach people about step six.

In the secular recovery version of the rock parable, three friends are sailing across the bay to the Island of Serenity.

One of their friends has missed the boat and the woman starts running toward it and wading into the water. They encourage her to swim, telling her that she can still catch the slow-moving boat, but every stroke she takes seems to put her further behind. One of the people on the boat notices her pockets are bulging, and yells, "Drop the rocks, and then you can swim!" It's not until she empties her pockets of the stones of self-pity, anger, intolerance, resentment, and fear, that she can make it onto the boat and reach the Island of Serenity.

Many people hold onto those same rocks, those burdens of self-recrimination, and it keeps them stuck in the same patterns, sometimes leading to a relapse. Step six is all about learning to drop the rocks—the things that weigh you down spiritually and emotionally—and then finding the lighter, happier life that waits on the other side. In the Bible, Proverbs issues stern warnings about what happens to people who don't find their humility, but also expresses some hope if they do: *When pride comes, then comes disgrace, but with humility comes wisdom.* (Proverbs 11:2)

When Vance was drafted by the Denver Broncos, he became an instant celebrity, adored by tens of thousands of people. He had wealth, women, cars, homes, recognition, and praise—all things that fed his pride. The alcohol and pills masked his doubts and the guilt, yet ultimately brought him to total ruin and disgrace. While working at a treatment center in Florida, with his bus pass in hand, he began to learn humility. He routinely gave up his seat to women, children, and the elderly. He would thank God for the smallest of blessings. He stopped judging people who shopped at dollar stores or discount markets and started seeing the world in new ways. This, in turn, allowed him to talk to the other people at the treatment center and give back to those who had helped him in his recovery.

Partly out of loneliness, partly out of his need to learn, and partly because he was genuinely interested in people outside himself, Vance began to talk to almost everyone he met. He often sat in the seat behind the bus driver, a man Vance's age who was also in recovery. The bus driver looked at Vance's muscles and said he wanted to look like him. Vance looked at the driver, and said, "I want to be like you. You have a full-time job. I just pass out balls."

His social life became the treatment center. Even though he was only paid for twenty hours a week, he often spent sixteen to seventeen hours a day there, listening and sharing. "Whenever I heard someone's story, I heard *my* story before I got treatment. I could relate to the men who had gotten divorced, the people who had lost loved ones, the people who became totally broke."

On the outside of the process now, he saw his own recovery through new eyes. Those in treatment often complained that the therapists were cold and unfeeling, but Vance saw it differently. "People don't get into that profession because they need a job. They get into that profession because they care. I rarely met a therapist who was just in that business for a job. The therapist has to be very honest with you so, as a client, you hated them. They had to tell you the things you never wanted to listen to before."

> "Whenever I heard someone's story, I heard my story before I got treatment."

He did that with a set of fraternal twins. Ray and Bryan Fodor grew up in New Jersey. In their mid-twenties when they checked into treatment, the brothers had been using heroin and pills since they graduated high school. They'd made one small attempt at getting clean, but it hadn't stuck. "We both knew that the only way we were going to get clean,"

Ray said, "was if one of us went into treatment and the other one did, too."

Ray took the leap first, checking into the recovery center on the fourth of April. His second day there, he was sitting on a bench in the gym when a stranger came up to him. "I didn't know him at first. Then he introduced himself, and I was shocked." Vance Johnson, former Denver Bronco, and fellow addict. "We talked and found out we had so much in common in our stories and our recovery."

Ray's brother Bryan followed him into treatment four days later. When Vance met Bryan, he thought he was Ray at first. As he had with his brother, Vance hit it off with Bryan, too. The three just clicked, as the Fodors put it, and the three talked every day of their forty-five day stay. "Vance's story and his passion about helping me and my brother helped get me on the right path," Bryan said. "He had a totally different why for being there, but his story could have been my story. That, and his spirituality, was what we needed. We believed in Jesus and the Bible, but connecting with someone on a spiritual level was what we needed to get through it. Vance took us under his wing, and he got us through it."

The twins, whose nicknames are Red and Blue, still keep in touch with Vance. He looks at them as sons and they look at him as another father. Vance helped put the wheels in motion, but the Fodors' parents and their older brother all helped with their recovery once they got home. "Vance wasn't going to be there every day, but our family was, thank God." Bryan said. "We looked up to Vance and we didn't want to fail him."

Both Ray and Bryan now have five years of sobriety. They work as retail managers and have both become fathers. When you ask them about Vance's influence, they are grateful and honest. "He's been a role model in my life," Ray said. "Seeing what he is doing, how far he has come, and where he was at in his deepest and darkest places in his life—he's my go to in my life, my sponsor, and another father figure. Honestly, if Vance hadn't been there on day two, I would have been checking out on day four."

Like Vance had almost a year before, many other men wanted to leave treatment. He became "the blocker", stopping them at the door. Vance was used to being part of a team, so to him, this was just team strategy. When he was at work, he'd try to bond the strongest guys into a band of brothers. "Any team naturally gravitates toward the strongest team leaders, whether they're a positive or a negative influence. I wanted to be that positive."

As the months passed, Vance's ability to relate to and talk to the other guys was noticed by the upper management at the center. When their weekend therapist quit, they asked him to lead the men's group on Saturdays. "I told them I had no training as a therapist. How was I supposed to know what to do? They said again, 'Just be Vance.'"

Vance Johnson, #82 for the Denver Broncos, had a job on the field during his ten years in the NFL. As a wide receiver, he had to do more than just catch a pass and run for the end zone. He had to know the plays and, most of all, know his opponents. "You have to know their weaknesses and strengths so you can capitalize on their weaknesses. You had to be pretty tactical, because some of those guys we were playing against were really tough."

> "Any team naturally gravitates toward the strongest team leaders, whether they're a positive or a negative influence. I wanted to be that positive."

For instance, Albert Lewis, a defensive back for the Kansas City Chiefs, became a friend of sorts with Vance. "I knew his wife's name and his kids' names. When we were out on the field, I would ask about his family. I'm not his friend exactly, but he's also not as aggressive with me because we have some kind of relationship now. I only needed one or two good plays against him to win the ball game."

For the first time in his life, he could see a brighter destination and he was determined not to veer off course.

Now, with his NFL days long behind him, Vance was back to using the same game-winning strategy, only this time with authenticity. He would go into the center, talk to the guys, and build that relationship. He got them to open up, discovered their strengths and weaknesses, and most of all, got them to drop their defenses. Many of the men in that treatment center were former professional athletes, just like Vance. He spoke their language, he knew their histories, and because of that, he could talk to them in a way no one else ever had.

Once he had that relationship established, he could begin to encourage them to drop the rocks weighing them down. Month by month, Vance discovered he was doing the same thing, and the lighter life he was leading—in all respects— was getting him closer and closer to the island. For the first time in his life, he could see a brighter destination and he was determined not to veer off course.

Seven

Restore

Brothers and sisters, I do not consider myself yet to have taken hold of it. But one thing I do: Forgetting what is behind and straining toward what is ahead.
– Philippians 3:13

In high school, Vance was a small kid. Wiry but fast, and also no match for the giants on the opposing teams. Vance had a fire in his belly to succeed, to be the best at everything he did. He always charged down the field, knowing that if he ran fast enough no one could catch him or hit him—something he avoided as much as possible after being injured twice, once breaking his arm. Touchdown after touchdown, Vance dominated the high school stadium. "I would play my heart out whenever I heard that a college scout was coming to watch some other team's star player. One time, I caught a punt on the thirty-five-yard line, then ran back and forth— from sideline to sideline—getting everyone tired and running into each other, trying to keep up with me. Then I blew through the group and ran all the way for a touchdown. It was said that I ran over one hundred and fifty yards on a one-hundred-yard football field that day."

Whatever Vance did, from art to football, he did to the best of his ability. He was always chasing that elusive goal of making his father proud of him, but the moments when his dad was happy were few and far between. Sometimes he would see his father on the sidelines, and as Vance would jog past him, heading back to the bench after scoring yet again, his father would call out, "Four touchdowns? Make it five."

> "The only thing that got through to me was people being hard. People literally telling me, 'You are crazy. You destroyed everything.' You couldn't nice me into being sober."

The message: *Never good enough. Never fast enough. Never strong enough.*

That criticism, however, was part of what fueled him. From the day he was born, Vance was on a mission to prove himself worthy, not just of his father's love, but also worthy of his coaches' and teammates' respect. Most of all, he wanted to be able to respect himself because he always felt like he could run faster, go further, and do better. "The only coaches who could get through to me were the ones who would rip off my head and crap down my neck. They had to break me down to build me up."

That all shifted with stardom, money, and indulging. By the time he made it to treatment, the celebrity lifestyle of a former Bronco gave the impression—both to his friends and to himself—that Vance was untouchable because everyone around him had enabled him, sucked up to him, and told him he was great. He didn't see the truth about himself, not at first. Not until the therapists were direct and devastatingly honest. "The only thing that got through to me was people being hard. People literally telling me, 'You are crazy. You destroyed everything.' You couldn't nice me into being sober."

The residual effect of all this direct honesty was a crushing weight of guilt. "Even today, I have lots of days where I am so broken that I just end up on my knees, crying out to God. Whether it's the loss of my son or remembering all the people I have hurt, all that pain breaks me. Everything I felt and went through was what made me break the hearts of people who loved me. I'll spend the rest of my life trying to make up for that."

Hebrews 5:8 reads, "Son, though He was, He learned obedience from what He suffered," This has been true for Vance ever since he woke up to the truth about his life. "I was so self-centered about the gifts the Lord gave me, and as a result, I filled my life with fleshly desires. Instead of seeing that if I cut myself off and starved my flesh, I could learn that I didn't need to feed that to myself." The selfish, lustful choices he made created the suffering, instead of easing it. He filled the holes in his heart with alcohol, prescription medications, cars, houses, women—pretty much every wrong thing he could choose. Hitting rock bottom and then choosing sobriety took all those things away and left him like Adam in the Garden of Eden—naked beneath God's eyes. Now, finally, Vance was brutally honest with himself. If he hadn't had God in his life, Vance realizes he would have gone right back into his addictions.

Putting his life back together was a struggle. His kids had stopped talking to him and cut off all communication. His friends had abandoned him, his family was done with him. His parents were the only people still in contact with him, but the relationship with his father was still troubled and difficult, if not almost impossible. Vance worked at the treatment center for almost a year and a half, spending almost every waking hour there, working with the other guys, learning more about himself, and concentrating on his sobriety. But at the end of the day, in the quiet of that one-bedroom home, the past came back to haunt him.

Then there was the grief. For years, he had numbed his grief over Vaughn's death with pills and alcohol. Numbed it to the point of being in a coma. His family was almost forced to decide whether or not to turn off life support. Some deep-seated will to live brought Vance back to life, but that life came with accepting and facing the devastating loss that haunts him every single day.

After he got sober, Vance went back to the cemetery to try to find Vaughn's grave, but couldn't. He'd been too high the day they buried his son (too high to speak, too high to be part of the funeral) and couldn't remember the location of his son's final resting place. This time, with his current wife and his five-year-old adopted son and nine-year-old adopted daughter, he returned to the cemetery. They drove around and around for about an hour. He saw a section where a lot of young children had been buried, but that wasn't where Vaughn was.

"We all got out of the car and took different sides of the graveyard to search. I was determined to look at every name on every grave. There were hundreds and hundreds of graves. My adopted son came up to me and asked if he could help me find his brother. What amazing words out of this little boy's mouth, who was ironically conceived the week my son was killed."

Vance told his son to look for V for the first name, and off the five-year-old went, calling out, "Daddy, Daddy," every time he found a V name. "I'd run to it, crying and excited on the inside but laughing too, trying to make it fun for him. After about three or four hours of searching, I was dying on the inside because I couldn't find it. I gave up and we started to drive out of the cemetery. My wife saw a grave digger and told me to ask him if he knew the location." Vance parked the car and asked the man if he could help him find his son.

The cemetery worker recognized him. "Hey, you're Vance Johnson!" Vance said yes, he was, but all he wanted was to find Vaughn Edward Johnson, not to talk about his career or his past. The worker called the office on his radio. A few minutes later, the information came back.

Vaughn Johnson, Vance Johnson's son, was buried at plot three, row thirteen. Vance's birthday is March 13th and his favorite verse in the Bible is the one that opened this chapter, Philippians 3:13. If Vance needed confirmation from God that he was on the right track, that moment was it.

He stood at his son's grave and said the words he'd held in his heart for so long. The grief poured out of him—honest and raw but, in a way, it lightened his burdens. Vaughn was gone, but Vance was there, sober and vowing he would never, ever, *ever* let another young man feel unwanted, unloved, or unsupported. His family joined him, all holding hands as they prayed over Vaughn's grave.

> *If Vance needed confirmation from God that he was on the right track, that moment was it.*

Later, Vance's five-year-old son said he saw a shadow pass over them as they prayed. Vance hopes it was his late son saying he knew his dad was there.

For years, Vance had prayed, and hoped, and begged for a way to make everything right again. Yet, at the same time, he felt unworthy of God's help because he had strayed so far from the right path. "It wasn't until I went to treatment to get away from *me* that my eyes opened. That's when I saw that all the prayers and crying out to God during my addiction had actually not fallen on deaf ears. God was there all along."

In Isaiah 57:2-6, the Bible says, "Those who walk uprightly enter into peace; they find rest as they lie in death. But you—come here, you children of a sorceress, you offspring of adulterers and prostitutes! Who are you mocking? At whom do you sneer and stick out your tongue? Are you not a brood of rebels, the offspring of liars? You burn with lust among the oaks and under every spreading tree; you sacrifice your children in the ravines and under the overhanging crags. The idols among the smooth stones of the ravines are your portion; indeed, they are your lot. Yes, to them you have poured out drink offerings and offered grain offerings. In view of all this, should I relent?"

> *Every time he stumbled, every time he felt weak, Vance got on his knees.*

Vance readily admits that he was that man of transgression, living a life of deceit, hiding from God behind pills and alcohol. But as he continued in his recovery, he kept his Bible nearby and continued going to church and maintaining an open dialogue with God. Like the rest of Isaiah 57, Vance was wearied by the length of his journey. It would have been so easy—too easy—he acknowledged, to quit right there and tell himself he had ruined too many lives and gone too far to return.

Instead, he followed Isaiah 57:10 and 13, "…you would not say, 'It is hopeless.' You found renewal for your strength, and so you did not faint…But whoever takes refuge in Me will inherit the land and possess my holy mountain."

Every time he stumbled, every time he felt weak, Vance got on his knees. For too long, he had done as Isaiah 57 warns, he made God into what he wanted, not the truth of who God is. "That scripture talks about how we are adulterers, carry lucky charms, and have pictures and statues of fake gods around our homes. We have uncovered our beds and loved the nakedness of others. It talks about how we get tired and find new strength in another relationship (as I did with yet another marriage) and replace God with that. None of this will profit us." If a woman argued with him or made him angry, Vance got a divorce and moved onto the next woman. If he lost a house to the bank or a car to the repo guy, he got another one. He kept moving on and replacing until there was nothing left, nothing but the detritus of his choices.

Those people, things, and substances helped him stuff his fears, anxieties, and worries into a deep, dark place. They delayed the inevitable reckoning that almost all people face as a result of their actions and choices. Another person, maybe one without the same deep faith Vance has, might not see a way through this. He knew where his answers lay—in the pages of his Bible. That book, the first book Vance read from cover to cover (and more than once), gave him everything he needed to complete his steps. "Our God offers comfort for the contrite. In the Bible, I found the comfort that I needed whenever I felt weak."

Vance kept on opening his Bible, learning about those who were broken and saved, and finding the answers he needed. Later in Isaiah 57, it says, "And it will be said, 'Build up, build up, prepare the road! Remove the obstacles out of the way of my people.' For this is what the high and exalted One says— he who lives forever, whose name is holy: 'I live in a high and holy place, *but also with the one who is contrite and lowly in spirit, to revive the spirit of the lowly and to revive the heart of the contrite. I will not accuse them forever, nor will I always be angry,* for then they would faint away because of me—the very people I have created."' That part about the contrite and lowly spirit really stayed with me. I wanted to be there, with God on my side, because that was the only way I was going to get through this."

So many times, while on the difficult road back to his life, guilt and regret often threatened to cripple Vance. He was incredibly contrite, but no one in his life wanted to hear from him, making any apologies or amends nearly impossible. So, Vance kept turning to the one person who would hear his prayers and stayed firmly on the path of his sobriety. It was the only way forward that he knew. Just like when he was on the football field in high school and dodging the defensive backs who were trying to stop him from reaching the end zone, he kept moving, even if it was only inches at a time, because he knew what waited on the other side was worth every single step.

> *Just like when he was on the football field in high school and dodging the defensive backs who were trying to stop him from reaching the end zone, he kept moving, even if it was only inches at a time, because he knew what waited on the other side was worth every single step.*

Eight

Amends

Everyone ought to examine themselves before they eat of the bread and drink from the cup. – 1 Corinthians 11:28

As a recovering addict moves through the steps, the process doesn't exactly get easier because the last half of the twelve steps is about facing up to and repairing the damage left in the addict's wake. The cheesy saying that is spoken at recovery meetings all over the world, "Keep coming back, it works if you work it," is true. Soon after leaving treatment, Vance realized that continuing to work and move forward in recovery was literally the only way through. He couldn't skip anything he didn't want to do, and he couldn't ignore any of the multi-layered parts of recovery. He had to, as he'd done on the field a thousand times, face every step with strength and grit. Getting to this point, step eight was all about being willing, because the hardest part was coming next.

Step 8: Make a list of all persons we harmed, and become willing to make amends to them all.

Even for the average person, making a list of people we have harmed is difficult. The kid on the bus you teased in middle school, the driver you cut off in traffic, the salesclerk you cursed out on a bad day, or the family member you hurt with cruel words. Every one of us has a list of people we have harmed in our past, but an addict's list is often much longer and widespread. Vance faced an uphill battle with this step because he couldn't remember large portions of the years he was using, so he didn't know where to begin his list. His children, his ex-wives, his friends, his teammates, his family—there were literally dozens upon dozens of people on his list. For a man who was used to dodging and avoiding his problems, whether it was his chaotic home or his marriages, making this list meant staying put and thinking about a painful past.

As a teenager, Vance ran away from home many times. One time, his parents spotted him walking the streets of downtown Tucson. "My father looked at me and asked, 'What are you doing way down here?' I said I didn't know and that it really didn't matter. He said, 'Well if you get hungry, you know where we live.' And they drove away." Vance was fifteen miles from home and only fourteen years old. He would run away, come home when it got cold, then run away again, trying to escape the fights and the fists.

> *Every one of us has a list of people we have harmed in our past, but an addict's list is often much longer and widespread.*

As an adult, he repeated that pattern. Ever since that one big fight with his first wife, Vance bailed out of every relationship at the first sign of trouble. "If there was an argument, I left. I got divorced. I moved on. I didn't want the same thing to ever happen again, so I ran away every time we argued." Instead of working it out, he put the relationship in his rearview mirror and looked to the next woman to fill the space beside him.

When his life began to fall apart and football lost its appeal, he didn't quit the Broncos. He simply stopped showing up. He'd been offered, and turned down, a million-dollar signing bonus to play with the San Diego Chargers. Then he was offered another three years with the Broncos. "I called them and said I'd be back and then I simply never showed up for training. Leaving football at that moment wasn't a hard decision. I had stopped seeing the joy, happiness, and fulfillment in the game. It had lost its value to me and, at the time, all I saw was my checks going into other people's pockets. The only joy for me with football was being on that field as a kid." On top of that, he wasn't at the top of his game anymore. He was using pills and alcohol heavily and had lost his starring role on the field. His passion for the game disappeared and, instead of confronting all that or answering to the team, he walked away.

His relationships with other people in his life had been turbulent as well. His best friend in high school thought Vance had slept with his girlfriend. He threatened to kill Vance, but even after Vance explained that nothing happened, the friendship couldn't be repaired. "That changed the trajectory of my relationships after that. I didn't trust other men and I didn't have another close friend until Mark Jackson."

Mark, one of the Three Amigos and another wide receiver for the Broncos, had been Vance's friend from the moment he joined the team a year after Vance. They were roommates during training camp and got along well. Then Ricky Nattiel was drafted the following year. Vance decided from the start that Ricky, who ran a 4.45 in the forty-yard dash, was not going to be deemed the best and fastest, so Vance ran a 4.35 in his tennis shoes, just to establish who was the better runner. Mark and Ricky became close friends, which left Vance on the outside.

Vance ordered a pizza, knocked on Mark's door, and asked him if he wanted to share. They watched the movie "Three Amigos" while they ate, and Vance told Mark the three wide receivers should dub themselves "the Three Amigos". Mark was sure it wouldn't work—especially since the actors in the movie were famous and white, and the three Broncos were black and, at the time, not so well-known. John Elway, the starting quarterback for the team, got on board and they all started referring to the three men as the "Three Amigos". "Mark, Ricky, and I became good friends because it forced us to get along to do commercials, speaking engagements, and signings together."

> *His amends list wasn't something Vance could avoid any longer, not if he wanted to continue his sober journey and become the man he should have been all along.*

Despite that, Vance made few real friends during those years. He had plenty of friends who would drink or party with him, plenty of friends who would ride his coattails, but not a lot of friends who would get in his face and tell him he was ruining his life. If people did try to do that, he cut them off because he didn't want to hear the truth. Then he drowned out their voices with more pills and more alcohol. Eventually, many people gave up and drifted away. Others remain hurt and bitter to this day.

His amends list wasn't something Vance could avoid any longer, not if he wanted to continue his sober journey and become the man he should have been all along. He didn't have his sister sneaking a runaway Vance food to make it easier. He didn't have a team to cover up for his mistakes. He didn't have someone waiting in the wings to stroke his ego and encourage him to ignore the heavy stuff. He had himself, his Bible, and God.

First, Vance had to become willing and open to the truths of his past. This is a process where the addict asks himself many questions: Were you kind and tolerant to others or mean and condescending? Did you lie and manipulate to get what you wanted? To cover for the addiction? Did you concentrate only on your own desires, regardless of the cost to others? Did you try to engender pity from others, instead of holding yourself accountable? Think of the moments you were insensitive or cruel, made promises you didn't keep, or let others down or let them take the blame for your actions. Then list every single one of them, as far back as you can possibly remember, detailing the person's name, what your actions did, what impact that had on the other person, and why or how you are responsible for those events.

One of the most important side effects of this grueling self-evaluation is maturity. By examining your own faults and admitting them to yourself, you gain a level of maturity that many people don't have. What that ultimately does is impact all future relationships because you learn to see the ripple effect of the smallest hurt—you yelled at the grocery store clerk, she in turn went home aggravated and yelled at her kids, so the kids were hurt and went to bed sad. On a larger scale, the hurts done to your parents, children, friends, and other loved ones can sometimes break apart families and drive the people you care most about into using as well. Vance has seen this with his own children, including one of his sons who has struggled with addiction and is currently in treatment.

According to a study in *JAMA Psychiatry*, a peer-reviewed journal published by the American Medical Association, children of addicts are *eight times more likely* to become addicts themselves. Couple that with the side effects of living with or being in a relationship with an addict—abuse, emotional withdrawal, codependency, attachment disorders—and a recipe for certain disaster is created. While making amends doesn't magically solve all of those problems or immediately repair the wounds of the past, honestly apologizing and demonstrating consistently reliable patterns of communication and contrition help the families of addicts to regain some stability.

To do this effectively requires total honesty. In the past, Vance's attempts at being open and honest had been limited. He'd been too worried about protecting his lifestyle and his own wants. In 1994, Oprah Winfrey contacted him after reading an article in the paper about Vance's argument with his wife—the one where she hit her head and passed out. He'd been on the front page of *The Denver Post*, his picture side-by-side with OJ Simpson's, in an article about abusive men. Oprah offered him the opportunity to come on her show and talk about what happened.

> *While making amends doesn't magically solve all of those problems or immediately repair the wounds of the past, honestly apologizing and demonstrating consistently reliable patterns of communication and contrition help the families of addicts to regain some stability.*

During the live show, Oprah asked him point-blank about that moment with his first wife. Vance broke down and came clean. He had sons and he knew that those boys, as well as all the impressionable young men who watched him play on Sundays, could turn out to be violent men. "I didn't want another woman to go through that, so I made a public apology in front of nine million people."

Oprah told him that she had a surprise for him and his first wife was suddenly live on a separate screen. Oprah asked her if she forgave Vance, and his ex-wife said, "No."

Vance knew that he had earned that no. He had been dishonest, he hurt her and his children by not being there. Instead of arguing for forgiveness, Vance said, "That's okay. I understand."

The bad publicity didn't help his career, and when he returned to the Broncos he was removed from the starting lineup. As his life continued to fall apart, that moment of honesty was lost and buried under a whole new set of lies, deceptions, and hurts. Vance's addiction was in control again.

Finally, almost twenty years later, Vance was not only ready for *things* to be different, *he* wanted to be different. Making this list forced him to confront the lies he had told himself for years. It forced him to see "the Vance" as a monster who had destroyed lives, not some harmless alter ego who liked to party. "The Bible calls us to die to ourselves. That actually was really easy for me to do because I was done with myself. I was literally dead to the old Vance. I think that's why I leaned on everything I read and heard in the scriptures. I made plenty of mistakes, trust me. That moral inventory convicted me when I did it, because it proved to me that I had been a liar."

When he walked out of that treatment center, Vance vowed to let his former self die and create a new life and a new self as he moved forward. He struggled, as anyone would— particularly in his relationships with his ex-wives, his children, and his father—but he kept seeking support and answers in prayer and the Bible. Doing that re-centered him at the end of the day and gave him the answers he needed.

"I have a saying: 'This life is a dressing room for eternity.' Meaning the life you are living now is preparing you for the everlasting life. You will pay the price for your choices, as the Bible says. Every step I've taken in my life was ordained to bring me to where I am now." When he looked at the pages and pages of his list of amends, he knew that apologizing and making up for the past would be a Herculean task.

Vance sat down, opened up his Bible, and searched for words that would encourage him in the hard days ahead. "In the scriptures, I saw so many broken people whom God had ordained, by allowing them to walk in a way that seemed right to them before they came back to Him. Just look at the Apostle Paul, who was a zealous persecutor of Christians while he was named Saul and before he found God. Paul called himself the center of all sinners because he persecuted and killed Christians and their families. And yet, Jesus appeared to him, someone so dark and who had hurt so many so badly. That sounded like my story and it gave me hope that I could be redeemed, too."

"Every step I've taken in my life was ordained to bring me to where I am now."

Vance was ready and willing to make amends. Whether those he had hurt were willing to hear those apologies was another story.

Nine

Repentance

Therefore, if you are offering your gift at the altar
and there remember that your brother or sister has
something against you, leave your gift there in front
of the altar. First go and be reconciled to them; then
come and offer your gift. – Matthew 5:23-24

The above lines from Matthew 5 are part of the Sermon on the Mount. Often misinterpreted as being simply about gifts to the church, they are really meant to represent the true sense of making amends. In this passage, biblical historians say Jesus is warning that simply going through the motions of reconciliation—by bringing a gift—is not enough. People need to make their amends face to face, with true humility, and then be reconciled.

In a recovery program, amends are made in person whenever possible because that requires courage and frank honesty. You can't dodge the truth with a text or a letter. Most of the time, the wounds were made face-to-face, so any apologies should be the same. Vance had lost track of or lost contact with many of the people he had hurt in the years he was using. His son

Vaughn was dead, his ex-wives and his children had cut off contact almost entirely. So, he started where he could—at home, with his mother.

And his father.

When he came home from treatment, his parents told him they were glad he was alive and doing well, but the arguments with his father and the history there was difficult to undo. "All I can remember, ever since I was little, is seeing my mom with black eyes. She covered them with sunglasses that she wore to work. She had cuts and bruises, and still went to work every day at the power company or the grocery store, back when we lived in Tucson. I had so much hatred in my heart for my father in those days. I hated seeing him come home at two in the morning, screaming at her because he was hungry. I hated how he didn't care about me. I hated how, if I was losing at a track meet, he would just get in his car and drive away. I just hated him."

When Vance was using and his parents came back into his life to run the restaurant, that hatred came out "full throttle", as he described it. "When I got my first Super Bowl ring, I put it in his hand and said, 'Here, this is for you.' He looked at me and said, 'I want another one.' Nothing I did was ever good enough." And still, when his father visited, Vance would pull out all the stops, flying his dad anywhere he wanted to go or handing over the keys to his Porsche. Their relationship remained rocky, with screaming matches and long weeks of nothing. "I hated him even more after my career was over because all I could do was reflect on my life and blame him for everything."

They would have loud, volatile fights at the restaurant, sometimes threatening to kill each other. One time when his father was screaming at his mother, Vance walked over, picked his father up, and then carried him through the entire busy restaurant and tossed him out the front door. "One day I recorded this huge argument I had with my dad. Later, I sat back and listened to all two hours of this fight where we are just screaming awful things at each other. In the last two minutes of the fight, I heard him say, 'This is not the son I raised. You need to get out of here, you need to get some help. You can't come back here again.' Out of the two hours of fighting, that's the only part that I remembered. That's what stuck with me when I went to treatment."

Years of buried hatred is difficult to erase, and Vance struggled with his feelings toward his father during counseling sessions at the treatment center. The therapists encouraged him to forgive the people who had hurt him because it was the only way to move forward toward ultimately forgiving himself for all he had done. He warred internally with the thought of releasing his festering bitterness and hatred. "My therapist talked to me and told me I had to forgive my father. 'Your father isn't suffering because of this anger,' he said, 'you are.'" It was true. Hatred and anger was tearing Vance up inside, poisoning his thoughts and his recovery.

> "I heard him say, 'This is not the son I raised. You need to get out of here, you need to get some help.'"

"Then one day, when I was working at the center, one of the counselors came into a group meeting with a big bag of tennis balls. On each tennis ball she had written a word: Shame, Guilt, Condemnation, Anger, etc. She gave each person in the room a tennis ball to hold. Then she told each of us to give a specific person our ball. Each of the people in the room came up, putting a tennis ball in the chosen person's hands. A hundred people were at that treatment center at any given time, which meant there were several dozen tennis balls to share. By the time everyone was done, that person's arms were full and people were putting the tennis balls under his arms, his neck, or in the crooks of his elbows.

The therapist stepped back and said to the man with the dozens and dozens of words and tennis balls, 'Which one do you want to get rid of first?' But his arms were so full of Guilt, Anger, Resentment, and Judgment that he couldn't see any one particular ball, much less drop it without having to let go of others. After a while, he got tired of holding all those balls. The therapist said, 'Do you want to drop all the balls?' When the guy said yes, she told him, 'That's exactly what you have to do.' So he dropped the balls and they bounced away, under the chairs, past the tables, across the room. They were gone because he had let them go. That lesson stayed with me long after I stopped working at the center."

> *"Even after everything that we had been through, I still loved my father. I loved him so much."*

He knew he had to let go of those emotions and hurts, so Vance called his father and asked if they could talk. When he sat down to make amends with his father, Vance had a startling realization. "Even after everything that we had been through, I still loved my father. I loved him so much. I also realized my father had his own underlying issues that were never dealt with. That moment allowed me to reflect on how I had become worse than he ever was." It gave the two men a bridge toward reconciliation, although it would take time to fully mend fences.

When it came to making amends with his ex-wives and his children, Vance had nowhere to start. He didn't have any of their phone numbers and wasn't sure any of them wanted to hear from him. He also didn't want to just show up on his kids' doorsteps because they had drawn a line between him and them, and he wanted to respect that boundary.

Then a strange coincidence happened. Back when Vance had four months of sobriety and did a radio interview tour to coincide with the Super Bowl in early 2014, 90% of the radio stations he talked to refused to air the interviews because he was so young in his sobriety and statistically very, very likely to relapse. One station, however, did air the interview and Associate Pastor Jake Ishmael, from Thrive Church in Thorton, CO, heard it. He contacted Vance and asked him to share his testimony in front of the entire church. "He was so bold in his faith on the radio. I looked for a way to contact him and sent him a direct message on Twitter. I told him the Holy Spirit really wants to use you in a powerful and profound way," Ishmael recalled. He asked Vance to come and give a testimony at the church. Vance hesitated.

Without the liquid courage found in a bottle of tequila, Vance was back to the same shy kid who left his own birthday party. He hated being in the spotlight as a kid because he stuttered, his teeth were crooked, and he was often bullied. In fact, when his high school handed out the Best Artist and Best Athlete awards, Vance's younger sister went up and accepted them for him while he waited outside, too shy to go inside and be the center of attention. He knew, however, that this testimony was an opportunity to make his regrets public, and maybe make the first steps toward easing the wounds of the past.

"I was sure my exes wouldn't believe me or want to hear my apologies. My children had endured so much abandonment and neglect from me for so many years, I was afraid to even text them when I first got clean. So, I stood on the stage at Thrive Church and asked if anyone in the audience knew any of my exes or my children. A few hands were raised. I asked them to just pass on a message for me and then I got honest.

Really, really honest. I got on my knees and said I was sorry. That it was all my fault, and that none of them—not my wives, not my children, not a single person I knew—was at fault for any of the carnage, hell, abuse, and abandonment that I put them through. I said that, if I could do it all over again, I wouldn't leave them and I wouldn't be the person who broke their heart. I said it was my fault that my son was dead, that I took full responsibility for all the actions and all the distractions I put in my life. No one else was at fault, just me."

As he spoke, Vance wept and wept, while the story poured out of him and he made the apologies that were so long overdue.

Ishmael said it was powerful to watch. People who attended his public testimony were in two camps—those who revered the former Bronco player and the team, and those who were angry with him for the past. "He was worried about how people would receive him and how they would respond. But when he stood up there and saw people he knew, he thanked them for coming," Ishmael said. "He put it all out there in such a way that I hope people would hear him, forgive him, and understand that it was the addiction. He was a humble, broken man."

As he spoke, Vance wept and wept, while the story poured out of him and he made the apologies that were so long overdue. Afterwards, he didn't assume anyone would respond because he knew he had done too many things to be forgiven for. "I didn't expect a single person to forgive me. When I was in treatment, it had taken me a long time to understand what amends meant. But as I read my Bible, and talked to the therapists, I realized it meant to forgive everyone and expect nothing in return."

Expect nothing in return. Not so much as a *thank you,* an *I understand,* or an *I forgive you.* Vance went into this step "fully expecting everyone to hate me for what I did. But I also knew there was no way I was going to relapse, even if all of them told me to take a hike." When he faltered, Vance focused on his late son and used that as a compass to guide him. "Amends is about putting yourself up on the cross, like Christ did, and offering yourself and your apologies. Nothing more."

After he spoke, Vance met with people in the lobby, in the pastor's office, and outside the church. Some just wanted to say thank you or ask for help with an addicted loved one, but many had angry words for the former Bronco. "There were people who had seen him at his worst, people he had taken advantage of, people he had hurt," said Ishmael. "But he talked to them all. He didn't avoid any of it. He owned his mistakes, and I think a lot of people respected him for that."

Gradually, the phone numbers and contact information trickled in. Vance reached out through social media and by texts to his ex-wives and his children, but many of them still refused to talk to him. It was a difficult process, one that was particularly tough for his current wife who sometimes doubted his intentions. "I understand how hard it is to marry someone who has been through so many relationships and how difficult it was to see me contacting those people from my past to make amends for hurting them."

Grace, mercy, and forgiveness. Those were the words he repeated in his head when people hung up on him, or refused to return his calls, or berated him about the past. There were doubts about his sincerity, questions about his commitment to his sobriety, and some long-buried hurts that came to the surface, but Vance kept going down his list, one name at a time. "I truly believe the Lord wanted to show me the meaning of that verse in Galatians 6:7: 'A man reaps what he sows.'"

The seeds Vance sowed in his years abusing alcohol and pills were evident in the broken relationships that surrounded him. Knowing this penance was necessary, "…was the only way that I could stay sober and not want to relapse or go back to my old ways. I just kept surrendering myself completely to my faith, and my love in Christ."

It wasn't a Hollywood ending. It took many years for any of his children to talk to him, and even then most of them have yet to maintain contact. His ex-wives still hate him for what he did. Many people think he is only doing this for fame or recognition, not out of sincerity. "It took years and was a very tedious process, with a lot of pain, a lot of admitting my faults, and standing there and listening to people talk about the pain I caused them."

> *The seeds Vance sowed in his years abusing alcohol and pills were evident in the broken relationships that surrounded him.*

Those who have forgiven him and reestablished relationships, have done so because they have seen him walk his sobriety and believe he is sincere. "The main way I make amends is by living a life that is in truth. I reach out to those who have experienced or are living in the pitfalls of addiction. I do interventions, offer education, share, and most importantly, speak truth."

He has yet to completely forgive himself. Losing his son is still a source of deep guilt and regret, but Vance said it drives him to be a better father to his children now. To never, ever ignore them or not be there when they need him. In doing his step work, Vance says he has to trust and believe that God really did forgive him. "He forgets my sins and throws them away as far as the east is from the west. All I had was faith that God would remove all of this from me."

There's a verse in 2 Chronicles, 7:14, that Vance recites when he talks about amends. "If my people, who are called by my name, shall humble themselves and pray and seek my face and turn from their wicked ways, then will I hear from heaven, and will forgive their sin and will heal their land."

Even if those who knew him then don't quite trust in his transformation, Vance knows that he is a changed man. He won't go back to living a life driven by worldly desires because he has seen firsthand—and still does today—what that costs.

When Vance speaks, he tells the truth about his childhood and his relationship with his father. When he's done, people often ask him, "How's your relationship with your dad today?" To show them the power of forgiveness and true amends, Vance calls his father and puts him on speakerphone with the audience. "I tell him that I want these people to hear me tell my father how much I love him." For three years, whenever Vance told his father he loved him his dad didn't say it back. But now he does, and even if it's not as strident or mushy as Vance's words, he knows his father means those three words and that their relationship will continue to grow. "He has a lot of stuff he hasn't worked through, but that's okay. I love him, and I love my mother and sister, and I am so grateful that they were always there for me. My mother never stopped praying for me. And, I have to say, I am so very, very grateful for her prayers."

Ten

Inventory

If we confess our sins, he is faithful and just and will
forgive us our sins and purify us from all unrighteousness.
– 1 John 1:9

Recovering from addiction is a lifelong process, not just in the constant battle against the urge to use, but also with the need to maintain the new behaviors that changed your life. It's all too easy to backslide into old patterns of denial and complacency and, as a consequence of those behaviors, fracture the relationships the addict worked so hard to repair. Step ten is about taking a daily inventory—looking at your actions on a daily basis and then immediately acting on any wrongs or hurts you may have caused.

For Vance, that inventory starts and ends with prayer. He's often up before sunrise and starts every day on his knees, thanking God for the second chance at life and asking Him to be a guiding hand in the day ahead. It's a far cry from how Vance used to be and how he used to let his inner emotions control his reactions.

"When I was younger, I had the worst road rage. If someone cut me off, I'd pull up beside them, roll down my window, and challenge them. I'd end up driving ninety to a hundred and forty miles an hour, just to beat someone to a destination. I would wait for my father to do something just so I had an excuse to yell at him. I didn't forgive people then—I took my anger out on them." Now, he tries to exercise more patience, grace, and compassion with everyone he meets.

> "When you truly lay your issues at the cross, you can't and shouldn't do anything back to the people who hurt you. That's what surrendering is about."

That doesn't mean life is all roses and songbirds. A lot of people haven't forgiven Vance for the past—not just those he was close to, but their loved ones as well. He gets messages on his Facebook page from people accusing him of using his fame or being fake. He tries to take a deep breath and see their anger with compassionate eyes. "Everyone has a history, and everyone has problems. Nothing—no person, no word, and no event—will throw me off my journey and my walk with Christ. I can't hold grudges and I can't judge other people or throw things back in their faces just because they confronted me with things I have done. I don't blame anyone for being pissed off at me. Like Paul said in the Bible, 'I am the worst of all sinners.' I see myself as the biggest whore and the most horrible person out of everyone I know. I broke hearts, stole, lied, cheated, and hurt the people who loved me. Who am I to judge another person?"

He likens that attitude to the concept of being nailed to the cross. When Jesus was hung on the cross, He was powerless to lash out at those who taunted or hurt Him. "When you truly lay your issues at the cross, you can't and shouldn't do anything back to the people who hurt you. That's what surrendering is about."

The daily inventory accomplishes several goals: It forces you to look back over the last twenty-four hours and honestly evaluate your actions and choices. It also gives you a daily opportunity to make amends with those who are close to you. And it regularly reminds the addict of the steps he already accomplished to get to this point. By not letting things wait and fester, the addict avoids denial, relapse, and the inevitable chaos that comes in the wake of acting out. In essence, a daily inventory brings peace to a person in recovery, and that's what Vance most appreciates about his life today. It is imperfect and messy, but it has more peace than any single minute of the days when he was using.

A daily inventory also keeps a constant dialogue open with God. Vance said he has many accountability partners, but they're human. They have lives and aren't always available when he needs to lean on them. "My sponsor is Christ. I know He will always be there and all I have to do is call out to Him for help and strength."

It also requires observing your patterns. This was something Vance started in treatment and continued after he was done. With eight marriages in his past, he knew he had to do some serious self-evaluation, particularly in regard to relationships and life partners. "Pastor Todd White once said in a sermon, 'If you have a problem with this person, this one, this one, and this one—it's not them, it's you. *You're* the problem.' If I hadn't gone through my steps, I never would have realized that. Until I did, I blamed everyone else but me."

He realized every single woman he chose to go out with had the same kind of spirit and they weren't the right spirit for him. "I tried every type and flavor of woman. They were all the same spirit, just in a different person. And that wasn't the spirit that God wanted for me."

He prayed about it, and in those long months after treatment when he was lonely, he had been talking to seven different women, located all across the country. None of them felt quite right, though, and when he asked his friends which one he should pick, they said, "Do what you tell us to do—pray about it."

So, he did. He dropped to his knees and talked to God. "I heard God say, the right woman will be the one who says I sent her to you." Vance thought that was crazy—he had these other women he'd been talking to. Surely one of them was the right one. Instead, he decided to trust God. He shut down the social media page that connected him with those women and decided to wait for whomever God sent his way. "One day, my iPad rings and I see a message on there from a woman I had never met before. She said, 'You're never going to believe this, but God says I'm supposed to be your wife.'"

Vance was floored. He took a moment, then called her and talked to her. A few days later, he flew out to meet Michelle and her children. She had been through her own trials and shared her story with Vance. "I liked her a lot, but then I got cold feet. I left the house and headed out to my car to go to the airport." One of her kids stopped him and asked to call him Daddy. The simple request broke Vance's heart, especially because his relationship with his own children was still so strained and distant. "I got in my car and said, 'Really, God? This is what You want for me?'" After some time in prayer, he had his answer. Vance walked back in the house and told her to start packing because he'd be back for her and her children.

They've been married for five years now and Vance says this marriage, made while he was sober and dedicated to God, is the one that he had been searching for ever since he saw that teenage couple at the high school. Vance officially adopted her children and said doing that has given him another view of God— being an adopted child of Christ means you are loved just as much as any other child. "Everything He shows me through her and these kids, God is showing me, too, in who I am to Him. God wants me to return that gift by honoring my wife and loving her unconditionally."

Like any marriage, there are ups and downs, as well as struggles with past baggage. Instead of bailing at the first sign of trouble, however, Vance has had to learn to stay and work it out, drawing on the lessons he learned in recovery and in the Bible about being a Christ-like partner in a marriage. The main thing he tries to do is make sure his wife knows that he loves and exalts her, in good times and bad.

For Vance, though, it means something deeper because he is committed to having a relationship that is based on God's eternal love. On Vance's Facebook page, he has a video about the difference between regular water and the living water found in Christ. "That's the kind of love we want—the living water of our Heavenly Father because it never runs out. Regular water leaves you thirsty later, and eventually you don't have a rope long enough to bring the water out of the well. But if you trust in God and His love, that living water never runs out and always fills you."

Living that way means letting go of past hurts. Sometimes that requires a daily lesson in grace. When Vance looks at his relationship with his father, he likens those years of hatred and animosity to an allegory about a snake in a house. "The snake is slithering through the house and knocks over a shaker of salt. The salt shaker breaks and cuts the snake, so the snake gets angry. It turns around and wraps its body around the broken salt shaker, squeezing and squeezing the sharp glass, trying to hurt it back. The glass doesn't feel anything and, because it's broken, it cuts the snake. The snake eventually squeezes so hard that it bleeds to death. Being angry at my dad—or at anyone—does nothing but hurt me in the end. It's time to let go of the salt because it's killing you, not them."

At the end of every day, Vance finishes his daily inventory by returning to prayer. He has a conversation with God about his day, about the things he is grateful for and the things he needs forgiveness for, as well as those he needs to forgive. "I believe in what the Bible says about forgiving those who trespass against you. That is what we are tasked with doing if we are going to live in and with Christ. That's the kind of life I've been looking for ever since I was a little boy, and now that I have it, I'll do whatever it takes to keep it."

> *Being angry at my dad—or at anyone—does nothing but hurt me in the end.*

Eleven

Seeking

Give, and it will be given to you. A good measure, pressed down, shaken together and running over, will be poured into your lap. For with the measure you use, it will be measured to you. – Luke 6:38

But seek first his kingdom and his righteousness, and all these things will be given to you as well. – Mathew 6:33

Martin Luther King, Jr. once said, "Faith is about taking the first step, even when you can't see the whole staircase." Vance has walked blindly into the next chapter of his life more than once, especially in the days since he got sober.

When he was a freshman in college and qualified for the NCAA college championships in Provo Utah, he was on the final day of the meet, and was the fifteenth-place qualifier. They only took the top fourteen. When one of the guys got sick, Vance took his place. "The great Olympian Carl Lewis was in first place going into the final rounds. The night before, I had a huge headache and I called my mom to ask for prayer. She prayed and I spent all night praying to God, asking Him to take away the pain. I also prayed that I would jump for Him the next day in the finals. On my last jump, I backed up an extra step so that I wouldn't foul. Then I took off running down the runway. At the last second, I realized that I was going to be short on my takeoff, but with faith, I jumped anyway. When my body flew into the air everything went silent; it was like I was running in the air. Everything seemed to be in slow motion. Then I hit the sand and heard everyone gasp. They measured my jump—26'11 3/4 inches. I had won the NCAA long jump championships and did it on faith."

It wasn't until he was in that canyon that he found God again and, a few months later—on faith—got on the plane and went to treatment.

He forgot his faith and connection to God when he reached the NFL. His life became focused on the next pill, the next drink, and the next woman. It wasn't until he was in that canyon that he found God again and, a few months later—on faith—got on the plane and went to treatment.

"I never stopped praying for you." Vance's mother said those words to him soon after he came out of the coma that nearly killed him and later finally got sober. The mother he had seen on her knees every single day, even while she was caught in the chaos of domestic violence, had put her faith in God to save her son, day after day after day. She prayed for her daughter, and she prayed for her husband and her marriage. Even though their marriage is far from perfect, Vance's parents have now been married over fifty-seven years.

His mother was the one who told Vance to turn to God when he had to make a difficult choice. Even today, she reminds him that all the answers he needs are there in God's hands, and all he has to do is ask for wisdom, then act on that wisdom with faith.

In recovery, addicts are encouraged to put faith in their Higher Power, whether that is God or something else, and to spend time in prayer and meditation. The addict's brain is often filled with the chaos of the crazy years before and the self-recrimination that haunts them for a long time as they move through recovery. Using prayer and meditation is a powerful way to stop those voices and to re-center, as well as maintain health and focus. Scientists have long studied the effects of prayer and meditation on the brain and on health, and several studies have seen a correlation:

> *For Vance, prayer has become an integral part of his life. It helps him keep his focus on what's important, dramatically reducing his stress and anxiety.*

- The National Institutes of Health did a study that found people who prayed regularly were 40% less likely to have high blood pressure than those who didn't.

- Dartmouth Medical School did a research study that showed patients who were religious and prayed before and after undergoing elective heart surgery were three times more likely to recover.

- The *Journal of Gerontology* surveyed 4,000 senior citizens and discovered those who prayed and meditated coped better with illness and lived longer than those who didn't.

- The National Center for Complementary and Integrative Health cites several studies that prove that meditative practices reduce stress, anxiety, and side effects of illness.

For Vance, prayer has become an integral part of his life. It helps him keep his focus on what's important, dramatically reducing his stress and anxiety. "When I cried out in the valley the day I hit rock bottom, I was literally turning back towards my roots and the belief system that my Mom gave me. I kept saying, 'Please hear me and help me if You are real.' I didn't know at the time that He had heard me. I just know my heart and my rock bottom was so profound, and I was just so broken, that connection with God literally was the only thing I could feel inside me that was real."

Ever since that moment, Vance stopped trying to steer his own life because that hadn't gone so well the first fifty years. Vance decided to trust in God and follow whatever path He put him on, regardless of the money he earned or where he lived or what he was doing. He found the more he relied on God, the less he desired the women, the pills, the alcohol, and all the things that had ruined his life and his relationships. "I made tons of mistakes during my journey, but He took away my need to cope with alcohol and pills as I found myself in Him."

He held onto a Bible when he was in treatment and read from it every single day. When he was young, Vance had gone to church and seen the Bible in his mother's hands, but never really delved into the Word of God or understood the messages inside its pages. As he grew in his recovery, he kept on reading his Bible and learning more about himself and his recovery every day. "When you are new in Christ, you can only take small sips of milk. But as you read more, discover more, and open yourself up to His message more, you can digest more. Then His spirit fills you and becomes the basis of everything you do."

Bryan Fodor said that he and his brother needed the faith that Vance had when they were in recovery. "Vance's belief in God and his faith were exactly what we needed. That was one of the biggest things, connecting with someone on a spiritual level, because that's what we needed to get through treatment."

Vance has focused on a specific Bible verse during each stage of his life. Some verses have taken on new meaning in light of his recovery and everything he has experienced. "I have several that I see now with new eyes, as I read and learn."

- *But if a wicked person turns away from the wickedness they have committed and does what is just and right, they will save their life. Because they consider all the offenses they have committed and turn away from them, that person will surely live; they will not die.* –Ezekiel 18:27-28

- *Let us examine our ways and test them, and let us return to the Lord.* – Lamentations 3:40

- *After I strayed, I repented; after I came to understand, I beat my breast. I was ashamed and humiliated because I bore the disgrace of my youth.* – Jeremiah 31:19

- *Everyone ought to examine themselves before they eat of the bread and drink from the cup.* – 1 Corinthians 11:28

- *He has filled the hungry with good things but has sent the rich away empty.* – Luke 1:53

When he came up with the title for this book, Vance said he drew from what the Bible had taught him and everything he had learned from God, especially from John 3:30 (there are those threes again) and the wisdom in this simple verse: *He must become greater; I must become less.*

Vance lost everything—every dime he had, every home he bought, every car he drove, virtually every person in his life, and almost life itself—before becoming far, far less than the superstar Denver Bronco who broke records and surpassed expectations. He entered the NFL thinking that God had given him the gift of athleticism so he could be a success. He'd make tons of money, live a life dramatically different from the way he grew up, and celebrate that talent every single day. That same talent, and what he calls the wrong thinking about it, took all those things away. "The whole reason I won a gold medal at the Pan Am games, why I went to the Olympic trials, why I went to three Super Bowls, was so that I could have a mighty fall. I was completely broken and now God is able to use me."

He likens his past to two stories in the book of John—the woman at the well and the demonized man. "How many times in your life have you been stuck because of the demons in your life? The mistakes you have made? I'm like that woman at the well who was married five times, and then later ran into the town and told everyone about Jesus and what he did for her. Jesus came and freed her, and she declared her belief to everyone she saw.

Here I am, a demonized man for most of my life, now free from the bondage of addictions. Why would I not declare that from the mountaintops? That's why I'm proud to say I was that man who was married many times, who was so caught up in pills and alcohol, who made all those mistakes, who was so stuck in those demons. Because Jesus took me out of there and filled me with Him instead. Christ gave me the hope of glory."

Losing everything, and the humility that accompanied it, taught Vance that nothing in the world mattered outside of God and what He provided. The former millionaire's most prized possession became a bus pass and a nine-dollar pair of pants from Walmart. The more he lost, the more he began to exalt God and hold Him up with gratitude and thanksgiving. He began to notice the flowers, and the sunshine, and the ordinary people around him. He—and Vance will tell you that this is key—stopped paying attention to himself and, instead, paid attention to others.

Because isn't that what God commands in the Bible? *Do nothing out of selfish ambition or vain conceit. Rather, in humility value others above yourselves* (Philippians 2:3). That lesson, Vance said, was the most important one he ever learned, and the one that has completely changed his life.

"It's simple Kingdom economics: Are you poor, are you hungry? Does the Bible promise you get to be full, rich, and in need of nothing? No. You get to be empty, because only in the emptiness can you find the true riches.

Job was the richest man around in the Bible. He was like Zuckerberg or Bezos or the President in today's world. Then he lost everything: money, homes, reputation, animals, even his children—all of them. In losing everything, he found out that God was enough. It's the same story with King Solomon who gains everything—money, fame, kingdom, women—and finds that gaining everything was worthless."

> *"Does the Bible promise you get to be full, rich, and in need of nothing? No. You get to be empty, because only in the emptiness can you find the true riches."*

All around us, Vance explained, are people who seemingly have it all, yet they are unhappy or lonely or struggling with bad choices. Some of those people end up pouring their money into addictions, which takes them away from the life and people they love. To Vance, this book is the next step in spreading the message that there is more to life—and a happy ending to be found—on the other side of addiction.

"You are in the middle of it right now, and maybe can't see your way out. But trust me, you can find a new purpose and life and restore all that you have lost. Maybe in a different way, but a more fulfilling and enriching way."

Twelve

Restoration

Brothers and sisters, if someone is caught in a sin, you who live by the Spirit should restore that person gently. But watch yourselves, or you also may be tempted.
– Galatians 6:1

When the crowds go home and the player hangs up his uniform, the emptiness in his life can be startling and financially devastating. An article done by *Kiplinger* discussed a *Sports Illustrated* study which found 80% of NFL athletes go broke within two years of retiring, and 60% of all NBA players face the same fate within five years. There are multiple reasons behind this—most athletes don't get courses in money management; they're young when they start receiving giant paychecks and spend the money foolishly; they think they'll be playing for many more years than they actually do; and many athletes have no idea what to do with their lives after their playing days are over.

Vance struggled to find his new career after he walked away from football. The different businesses he tried—real estate, trucking, restaurants—were not a good mix, and either he left them or they failed. His addiction blew through a lot of his money; debt and child support took the rest. He spent almost three years working at the treatment center with his fifteen dollar an hour job before taking a similar position at a different center. It wasn't the big money he used to make, but it was satisfying work that allowed him to help others.

In those years, the young man who was so terrified to speak that he skipped awards ceremonies and birthday parties, found that he had a calling—as a speaker. That first testimony, given at Thrive Church shortly after he got clean, became an annual trip, sometimes more than once a year. With Vance at the pulpit, people who never went to church before or who stayed away from church were showing up to hear the former Bronco, and people who have loved ones or are themselves in the deep cavern of addiction began finding hope and getting help. Thrive has become a recovery hub, Associate Pastor Jake Ishmael said, for people needing treatment. Their Recovery Road group meets five times a week, and Ishmael said it could meet twice as often and still not be enough. "To have somebody who was so loved and is still such a revered figure in Colorado is a big bonus. People come to see him and stay to listen to his story. He doesn't just speak and leave—he's there for the people who need his help. He's worked really closely with our church to help people get help, whether it's someone local or out of state."

The more he spoke, the more Vance realized the power of his words and that this could be a new career of sorts for him, one that spoke to his mission of living a life dedicated to Christ.

The more he spoke, the more Vance realized the power of his words and that this could be a new career of sorts for him, one that spoke to his mission of living a life dedicated to Christ. "My being here, talking to people today, was like a whole mixture that God put together, made up of all the things I had to go through, everything I had to lose, and all the lessons I had to learn. It was a recipe, and you just have to let go and believe that once it goes in the oven, God is going to make it cook until it's something perfect for you."

Just as he had with Ray and Bryan Fodor, Vance began helping as many people as he could. His Facebook page gets dozens of contact messages every day from people asking for guidance, interventions, prayer, and advice. Vance answers as many as he can every day. He keeps in contact with others he has helped, and their praise runs deep and gracious.

"After losing my job, my girlfriend, and almost my life, hope was all but a distant memory. I remember the feeling vividly when Vance walked into my room. My mindset shifted. I knew I was in the presence of someone special, who meant me no harm and could help me see something I was unable to see in myself. Having trudged the road of addiction for over a decade, I had encountered plenty of interventionists, motivational speakers, and otherwise perceived enlightened individuals. Vance was different. I could tell he truly believed in what he was saying, that he lived it. His words were not from a textbook or a weekend seminar at the Holiday Inn. They were the truth; his truth...My truth. From that day forward, I understood what I was capable of had nothing to do with my past failures. I understood that there was hope for me. The happiness was achievable. That my life was not over but was about to begin." – Isaac

"Where do I start? [When I went into treatment], I had no idea who Vance Johnson was nor did I care. I didn't care who anyone was at that point. I was doing what I was told I had to. One activity through the day was a class with Jorge and Vance. The oddest pairing of people, but it worked perfectly. Jorge would share all the medical and by-the-book fact stuff, then [Vance] would come in with the life experience side of it. The passion he had/has was mesmerizing. Drew me in like a magnet. The rawness and transparency that he shared was contagious. I also was fortunate enough to get picked to go through a program called Hero's Journey, which I believe is the reason I'm still sober today. It was a three-day intensive therapy. There was an exercise we did where…you confront people from your past [imagining they are sitting] in a chair across from you. Everyone else had their chair right up close to them. I had so much anger stored up, [my chair had] to be put across the room. The imaginary confrontation didn't go well, so Vance stood by the chair as if he was the person being confronted. He stood there and took all my anger and rage towards that person. Neither one of us could explain it at the time, but everyone in that room felt it. Later I also shared a letter I wrote to my father…basically just letting him know what I felt from how he did us. [Vance] and I were both in tears after he read it. Vance said it gave him a different perspective on his own situation. He had only seen it from the father's side, but now as he read my side, I could see things clicking like *oh shit I didn't think of it like that.*" — Luke

Just recently, Vance answered the call of a mother whose daughter, a mentally ill addict, tried to kill herself. In a weird ironic twist, Vance got pulled over for speeding, just as he had so many years before. But this time, his mission wasn't to get to a casino—it was to make a flight that would save this girl's life. "It's as if my entire life is being redone, but this time for the right reasons."

When the girl asked him why she should listen to him, he told her what he tells everyone who is where he was years ago—*because I was once you.* He told her about Vaughn, about how the loss of his son has become his why, and how he tries to help every single addicted person he sees, because that is his mission now. "My past is what has prepared me for this life. Every single thing I did as a child and as an adult were the same things I had to do with my faith and my sobriety."

When the girl asked him why she should listen to him, he told her what he tells everyone who is where he was years ago—because I was once you.

Not everyone he helps makes it. The Fodor brothers have helped several people, paying it forward from their own time in treatment. A few people have died instead of getting clean, which is heartbreaking and devastating for the person reaching out.

Vance said that when someone goes back to using, he drops to his knees. "I used to blame myself when I heard that people had relapsed or died. I would think, *if I just could have gotten to them sooner*...but as I continued to read the Bible and understand what Christ called me to do and be, I realized that the only thing any of us can do is encourage others. The Scriptures say we plant the seeds and water them. God is the one who helps those seeds grow."

He had to learn that he can't change or fix anyone else, only himself, and that the best way to encourage others to get sober is to live a life of sobriety and dedication to God.

He had to learn that he can't change or fix anyone else, only himself, and that the best way to encourage others to get sober is to live a life of sobriety and dedication to God. No one can be forced into a rock bottom, Vance points out. No matter how many people told him he needed to quit drinking and using pills, he didn't listen. He had to hit that bottom himself, in that canyon. "People have to be ready to hear the message and to receive it. It's the same as the soil. If the soil is not fertile, there is nothing that is planted in that dirt that will work. Hopefully I'm being used by God to plant a seed there."

To continue his recovery mission, Vance will be involved with the Blackberry Center in Florida and will be working at a newly opened facility in Las Vegas. Both facilities are part of Oglethorpe Recovery centers and will be open to pro athletes as well as ordinary people. Vance said having people on staff who were former pros is a necessary component of communicating with people like him. "They need someone who speaks their language. If it wasn't for Randy Grimes and watching his YouTube video about recovery thirty-three times, I never would have believed a pro athlete could get help and change. I am so grateful to him, and for all he did. He was the one who talked me into treatment when God cleared my ears."

For years, Vance was oblivious to the needs of others and the hurt his addiction inflicted on their lives. Now his eyes are open, and he said God has—as promised in the Bible—taken out his heart of stone and given him one of flesh. That heart hurts over the distance between himself and his children and the regrets from the past. "The Bible says we're supposed to put our hands to the plow and keep looking forward, not at what lies behind. If I look behind, I have no reason to be sober. I have to look forward and not hold myself in guilt and condemnation. There's nothing in that but death."

He is determined to live a life that leaves nothing to be regretted, and to always focus on what is most important. Vance often cites Bronnie Ware, a palliative care nurse and author of the book *The Top 5 Regrets of the Dying*. Her book points out that, when people approach the end of their lives, their list of regrets have nothing to do with making more money, working longer hours, or being in a different career:

1. I wish that I had let myself be happier.

2. I wish I hadn't worked so hard.

3. I wish I'd had the courage to live a life true to myself, not the life others expected of me.

4. I wish I'd had the courage to express my feelings.

5. I wish I had stayed in touch with my friends.

Vance adds a sixth to that list and would put it as the top regret. "My wish is that more people knew Christ because they're going to spend a lifetime apart from Him if they don't." Now that he is living his life in and for God, Vance said he is richer than he ever was in the NFL. He is more satisfied than he was with thirty cars and fourteen homes. "My life is full; my heart is full. And I owe it all to Him."

There's a moment that Vance returns to from time to time, kind of a placeholder for where he was and how far he has come. When he got to treatment, Vance said he was dead inside and couldn't yet see a way to another future. He'd lost himself, lost his humanity, and lost everything that mattered. "I remember standing in the Atlantic Ocean and looking out over the horizon. It was the first time I saw how wide open the world ahead of me was. That was the possibility of my life, if I got clean. Behind me, there were weeds growing out of the sand. That was the life I was leaving behind."

He bent down, picked up some shells and tucked them in his pocket so he would never forget that lesson. "Then I stared at the horizon for a long, long time. Because in that wide-open space, I saw hope."

About the Authors

About Vance Johnson

At the height of his career, Vance Johnson, one of the "Three Amigos" recruited by Mike Shanahan for the Denver Broncos, was hiding a serious alcohol and pill addiction that cost him literally everything he had. He hit rock bottom in the middle of a canyon in Colorado, and from that moment, began the slow journey of reclaiming his life and becoming the man he should have been all along.

The three-time Super Bowl wide receiver learned to be tough from early on, because he grew up in a home where domestic abuse was an everyday occurrence, and being the best was the only option. Vance was always searching for his joy, that one thing that would fulfill him. He didn't find it in his eight marriages, he didn't find it playing for the NFL, and he didn't find it within himself. The death of his oldest son, several suicide attempts and a 28-day coma brought on by his pill/alcohol abuses, combined to be the wake-up call he needed.

His memorable and unforgettable story is one that is almost too incredible to believe—but it's also that very truth that eventually set him free from addiction.

Now happily married and sober, Vance tours the country as a recovery ambassador for Oglethorpe, Inc., speaking and encouraging others who are at their breaking point to look to the power of God to change their lives. His book is an honest, raw account of the destruction brought on by addiction and the power of faith in finding the way back from the depths of hell. *Uncovered* is more than just Vance Johnson's unbelievable life story—it's a book of hope and a path to finding a brighter, better life.

Contact Vance at www.VanceInspires.org or www.VanceCares.com

About Shirley Jump

New York Times bestselling author Shirley Jump started her career as a journalist for major metropolitan newspapers in the Boston area. She is the author of seventy books, both fiction and nonfiction, including *Finding Level Ground: The Story of Matthew DeRemer*. She currently works as the Director of Publishing for NOW SC Press.

Visit her website at www.ShirleyJump.com

Resources

If you or a loved one needs help, please visit www.VanceCares.com.

For in-patient options, visit either the Blackberry Center in central Florida or the Vance Johnson Recovery Center in Las Vegas for information about targeted substance abuse treatment. Vance also serves as the Recovery Ambassador for treatment experts Oglethorpe, Inc. Founded in 1999, Oglethorpe's mission is to provide support for people who have lost hope, guiding them on a compassionate journey toward a better future. They breathe new life into failed or struggling psychiatric health and addiction recovery centers, providing up-to-date technology and equipment as well as training and oversight for all hospital staff members. Today, Oglethorpe oversees more than 1,200 employees at nine treatment centers throughout four states.

All Oglethorpe healthcare staff members are trained in providing a safe and caring environment, laying the foundation for patients to learn, grow and thrive. As an organization, they care for their staff members, facilities and, most importantly, the patients that they serve. Together, they provide support and hope.

If you or a loved one is struggling and is in need of behavioral health or addiction recovery services, the doctors, psychiatrists and healthcare staff of Oglethorpe are here to help. Visit their website, www.OglethorpeInc.com to find the hospital location nearest you, and to learn more about how Oglethorpe's treatment programs restore hope and light for those in search of a lasting recovery.

For speaking inquiries regarding Vance Johnson, contact: www.VanceInspires.org

For recovery help and information, call 888-82VANCE

Vance's mother and father
(age 16 & 21)

Vance and his sister
Tammy, his first time
playing football

Vance Johnson's Football Career